Contents

	FOREWORD	THE TITANIC	79
8	THE MIDWIFE	POUNDIES, KNOBS, CHAIN BONES	82
9	DELIVERIES	KHAKI	85
11	TWINS	THE DONKEY'S BACK	86
13	SIX NAMES	A RICKLE	87
14	GRANNIES	THE ELIMINATOR	88
15	GRANNY REILLY'S WEE SHOP	MICKEY WI' THE WINDMILLS	89
17	COWBOYS AND ONIONS	DANCING WITH THE BLOODS	90
19	THE GULLEY MAN	THE PENNY PICTURES	91
23	THE BEN WEED RACE	IRIS STEW	93
24	AISLING	THE WAKE OF THE GOAT	96
27	THE MENU	PARADISO	97
29	THE COOKS	JOSEPH LOCKE	99
31	THE BANNISTER	COLD TURKEY	100
32	THE DEANERY SCHOOL	HURRICANE DEBBIE	103
33	THE DEANERY EXCURSION	BILLIARDS	104
35	MR BEATTIE	THE MEDAL	107
36	SINGING SCHOOL	ARCHES	109
37	DANCES	BANDS	110
39	DRAWING THE LINE	THE BONE FIRES	112
41	THE BARS	THE FIFTEENTH	114
42	GOSSAMER	THE RABBLE	117
45	FATE	A FALLEN PALATE	119
47	BIG NIGHTS	SEVENTY-SEVEN	120
49	THE BRIDE BOAT	THE WATER CART	122
51	THE WAR	THE MANGLE	123
52	ALEPPO	THE RANGE	125
54	SIR BASIL	THE FALL OF BABYLON	126
55	GETTING RELIGION	AFTER BABYLON	127
56	ALAMEIN	THE WALLS	129
59	MEETING THE POPE	THE STREETS	132
61	MAGGIE	THE HALF MOONS	134
63	THE FLUTE	THE DARK LANE	136
65	BANANAS	THE HOLY PICTURE	137
66	GRANNY AND THE CUSTOMS	BREAKNECK	139
68	HOW TO SMUGGLE	GREY	140
69	SMUGGLING	BOG BEAN AND SULPHUR	142
71	WETTING THE TEA	THE BARBER'S	143
72	TOAST	SQUINCY	145
73	HALF A' DERRY	A SEVERE BAD NIGHT	146
75	THE FITTER	LAST RITES	149
76	BILLYCANS	CROSSING THE JORDAN	150
77	DEAD HORSES	SCARLETINA	152

Foreword

I've never liked History - it's so predictable, with its predictably constant wars and famines and droughts. And what I like least about History is that it has things *the way they are today*. Things today are not, as we all know, what they used to be in days-gone-by. They never are. In days-gone-by things were very, very good indeed. The hours were long, and you worked hard, but the summers were green and the days were golden. The people were poor but they were happy.

I like people, though. Individuals, ordinary people. And ordinary people, along with equally unpredictable phenomena like earthquakes and volcanoes, are the makers of History. They make it by being implicated in the events that are recorded in the History books. They are the ones who call people to arms, take up the call to arms; who starve and who feed the hungry; who die of thirst and who invent ways of irrigating the land. They make it too, just by living, by going on about their business, simply by being there.

The Fountain is a tiny, decaying estate between the Cathedral and the Foyle, clinging by its fingernails to Derry's Walls. Originally it was just one street running between Bishop's Gate and Ferryquay Gate, encompassing, later, the warren of tiny streets that branched out from it. Its people, staunch in their loyalist working class traditions, have held on in The Fountain through the wars, the recurring 'troubles' and what they regard as the insensitive re-development of the area in the late sixties and early seventies.

The effigy of Lundy is still made there. Bobby Jackson's famous mural of William crossing the Boyne, once so highly prized that it was air-lifted to a new location during the re-development, still stands at its centre. But there is a feeling among the older residents of the area that time is running short for The Fountain. Much of the original character of the estate has already been lost. The intimacy and neighbourliness of the narrow red-brick streets is long gone. Many of those born in the bedrooms of the terraced houses have moved out to new estates in the Waterside and further afield. The man who makes the face and epaulettes of Lundy is now in his eighties and thinking of giving it up. He has two of the papier mâché masks ready to keep the tradition going until someone can be found to take over. The garage doors that protected Bobby Jackson's mural from the elements were blown down in a night of wind some years ago. They were never replaced; the wood was broken up and used for bonfires; the mural is crumbling. The central building of the re-development, like a multi-storey car park with Economy Seven, will have been demolished by the time you read this.

For some time the older residents of The Fountain had been toying with the notion of writing a book about the estate. They formed a committee and approached Sam Burnside at his newly opened Verbal Arts Centre in the Cathedral School Building where many of them had been educated. Sam, enthusiastic about the idea, advised and encouraged them.

I had just been appointed one of the four Artists in the Community for the Arts Council and, as part of my work, was seconded to the Verbal Arts Centre, where Sam suggested that this was a project in which I could become involved.

During a walk round The Fountain he came up with the idea that a photo-essay might accompany the text we produced. I leapt, in my usual slow motion, at the suggestion. This book is the result of that conversation.

I regard the approach used to producing the text and the photographs as analogous. I tried to keep out of both as much as possible. For the photographs I adopted a single format, close to the dimensions of the negative and printed them as simply as I could, controlling only the composition, trying to be true to what presented itself as interesting and memorable. Similarly, with the text. The people told me what was interesting, memorable and important to them; I wrote down, as accurately as punctuation and the need for clarity would allow, the words people said and the way they said them. The text is, therefore, unashamedly anecdotal - and none the worse for that. It contains both the set pieces of the practised urban storyteller and the urgent recollection of good conversation.

My job as Artist in the Community was, it seemed to me, to be both visible and invisible. I needed to be there, and to be seen to be there, as a focus for the work that the people wanted to produce, and, at the same time, to intrude as little as possible on that work. The ultimate concern of the artist is to marry content, whatever that may be, and form. There was no shortage of content in The Fountain - nor is there, I am convinced, in any other community - and what was required was a form that would transmit that content effectively.

The oral form in which the content was given to me had an innate vitality, character, and rightness. Each conversation had its own dynamics. The major problem in producing the text for the book was that the rightness and dynamic of speech are not the rightness and dynamic of written prose. While, at first sight, the text might seem, in its layout, to have aspirations towards being poetry, it should soon become clear that it is simply a way of representing, accurately, the dynamic of conversation. Not that that means it isn't sometimes closer to poetry than Poetry.

I found, in trying to write this text, that the comma, the full stop and the semi-colon are conventions completely inadequate as equivalents for the spaces in the spoken language and the meanings they carry. It was brought home to me, in other words, that the written language, even at its best, is, in ways, a much less supple medium than the oral. What the written gains in the deliberateness of its composition - and these are the only words I can use here, because the oral language has just as much control, logic, clarity and purpose, though they are of an entirely different kind - it can lose in vivacity. It is difficult, if not impossible, and you can hear this every day on radio and television, for the best-educated and most articulate of people to *speak* entirely coherent prose. Orally we all get to our meaning by what a friend of mine calls 'single-minded swervings', and the negotiation between what we try to say and the performance our mouths and brains seem to manufacture between them to thwart us, the back-tracking and repetition and grunts and groans required, gives the oral language an entirely different structure from the written.

So the text of the book, *The Fountain*, is an *image* of the stories I was told, as different from the reality of what was said, and how it was said, as the frozen moment in black and white is different from the movement and colour beyond the camera lens. They are both snapshots - each limited in its way - but, if I have done my job, retaining at least a shadow of the unpredictable *éclat* of the original.

All the photographs are about The Fountain because they were taken in The Fountain. I have tried, where possible, to relate them to the text in a way that illuminates both. Because of lack of time and the exigencies of printing, among other things, I have not always succeeded. There is never any question of the text describing the subjects of the individual photographs. The man or woman in the photograph is *not* the character described in the text.

I am grateful to The Arts Council of Northern Ireland, for the opportunity to work on this project; to everybody connected with The Verbal Arts Centre, and, in particular, to its director, Sam Burnside, for his enthusiasm and advice; to the staff of the Central Library; to the staff of the Orchard Gallery; to all those who read this text in its many drafts; to the principals, teachers and pupils of all the schools involved, and in particular to Templemore and Clondermott, whose pupils conducted many interviews, to First Derry and Carlisle Road for allowing me to take photographs there; and to Cathedral and Long Tower, who, with First Derry and Carlisle Road, painted the mural; to the artist Neil Shawcross for, among other things, permission to reproduce the mural; to the Committee, and to the writers' sub-committee, from The Fountain and, above all, to the people of The Fountain themselves.

'I'll be perfectly frank with you.
They talk about the border now.
They talk about The North and The South.
But, basically - under the skin - we're all Irish.
It's immaterial whether we come from The North or The South.
There is a bond with all Irish people.
You go across to any other part of the world,
and when you hear a tongue, straight away, they're Irish.
You don't ask them if they're from The North or The South.
The Irish people gravitate to each other.
And, you see, this, to me, is a tragedy.
Because, whenever things happen -
you get something that really happens - when the war started
there was conscription in England and Scotland and Wales.
The people in Ireland, North and South,
didn't have to be conscripted.
There were people getting tortured, people getting murdered,
and, as a people, they went.
This, to me, is the tragedy of Ireland. People talk.
I have friends Catholic. I think the world of them.
I have no intentions of ever letting anybody do them an injury,
nor they'll not let anybody do me an injury.
We have a respect for each other.'

'I think a lot, too, is in the bringing up.'

The Midwife

'... and all the women had their babies at home.
Nobody went into hospital like they would do now
to have babies - they all had them in the house.
And the midwife -
word used to go up and down The Fountain...'
                                        'Mrs McGahey...'
'She was a qualified midwife, right enough,
she used to just - whenever they needed her -
they sent down for Mrs McGahey...'
                        'They would have had her booked...'
'They would have had to book her, and then
whenever the time came they would have sent
some of the youngsters or the husband
down to tell Mrs McGahey
to come up the mother wanted her.
And most of the babies were delivered at home,
and Mother's first two were twins - twin girls -
and she worked in Welch's, and she worked
that Saturday morning and she wasn't feeling very well
and she came home, and the twins were born the next day,
the following day - the Sunday.
And when Mother was out at work
I used to go into my granny - she was great -
an old woman with a black shawl - she was great,
and she used to have a plate of toast ready.
Coming in from school we went in to her, you know,
till we got a bit older,
and then we just went into our own houses...'
  'And every Tuesday she visited her sister. So she used to -
   she had a wee bracket in her kitchen - a wee corner shelf -
and she used to leave a ha'penny the day she wasn't there.'
'And we would have gone in and got our ha'penny
and away round for a ha'penny worth of sweets
and then sat on the windowsill, like,
waiting till she came in at five...'
                        'And I hated a Tuesday and the sweets.
            I'd rather have had the tea and the toast and the fire.
                        Everybody went in to a granny, y'know.
Most of the women worked and we went in to my granny,
                        because she would have had nobody.'
'We loved my granny...'
                        'And we stayed with her...'

Deliveries

'She delivered them here, and down in The Bog,
she delivered wains down in The Bog,
and many's a time all she got was a glass of whiskey.
But I remember hearing a story
that one night the door went at two o'clock in the morning
and it was some man from down the Lecky Road.
Now this was at the time of the Black and Tans
and there was a curfew and all the rest of it in the streets,
and he said,
"Nurse, my wife's in labour, could you come down?"
And she said,
"Go on you down, son, I'll get dressed and come down".
And apparently always put on the nurse's uniform,
almost like a clergyman or a priest -
she went into her professional role -
so the uniform went on to deliver the baby
and she was going down Fahan Street,
the old Fahan Street then.
And the police patrol - the Black and Tans -

9

And some of them had very little hot water -
you had to boil all the kettles of water, you know,
you had to go out into the kitchen and wash -
the scullery they called it -
and you had to just say, "Don't come out!"'
                                        'And an outside toilet.'
'And you just had to keep putting on kettles of hot water -
but if they had, we always say, if they had just built on out...'
                                'Fixed up the old houses
                and left everything the way they were -
        I think everybody would have been happy enough.'
'I think a lot of people would have been much happier...'
'They had to work harder, I think, to keep the houses clean
                        because there were very few carpets -
        it was all oil-cloth - no carpets - just oil-cloth and rugs.
                It was hard work keeping all these things clean.'
'And you had to scrub the fronts of the houses
and the half-moons...'
    'And you had to wash in a big tin bath with two handles
    and everybody kept a bucket for boiling their clothes in...'
'That's right.'
                                    'And a washboard.'
'A washboard.'

                        'Now they play them...'

Six Names

'My mother and father were both christened
on the same day
in the same font -the Cathedral -
and my mother didn't know it, naturally enough,
until she started -
in fact it was after she married my daddy
and they were up in my granny's
and she brought out the Church magazine -
she kept them - and there it was -
Charles Alexander
and Florence with her six names...'

     'You would never believe it -
      and was she proud of them!
    Florence, Letitia, Frances, McGonagle,
      Dorcas, Glynn Hamilton -
  my granny must have been spare. That's true.
  She must have went to call her for everything...
     They got her to say them on RTE -
      remember she was on RTE?
     And they got her to sing on it...'

'Augh, she was really great,
and she was really proud, you know.'

   'And she told me that when she was a wee girl,
     she said, like, times were really hard
  and she was wanting to get some money for my granny
  and she says she went round the factories to look for a job
     from about when she was thirteen.
   And she says she went to Hamilton's factory,
    and the man says to her "Well now,
  when will you be fourteen?" And she told him.
  And he says, "Well, I'll - if you come back
     when you're fourteen -
    just give me your name and address..."
And she said - she always did the same thing - she went,
"Florenceletitiafrancesmcgonag..." He nearly had a fit!
   She was really proud of it, you know.
    I said to my father one day,
   "Did you know that was her name?"
And he says, "Naw, not till the day that we got married
  an' if a'd known that a wouldn't a'married her!'
     He was affronted.
And most of the people in The Fountain knew about that.'

Grannies

'I'm sixty eight,
and do you know, I didn't know -
well I was nine -
and I remember my granny
with a long skirt and a shawl,
and to me she was an old, old woman,
and when my father died
Kathleen says to me,
"Just think, May," she says,
"my granny was the same age as my father
when she died..."
and I says,
"My granny? Are you sure?"
She says, "Aye, that's all she was".
I thought my granny was about ninety -
of course, when you're nine...'
                    'When you're nine everybody looks *ancient*,
                              everybody looks ancient.'
'But we must all have had the same ideas about grannies,
because I knew a hairdresser
and I met her one day getting off the bus -
I hadn't seen her for years -
and she'd married and had a few children
and given up the hairdressing and,
"Augh," she says, "May,
it's that good to see you!"
I says,
"Where are you running to
at this time of night? "
She says, "May,
I'm goin' up to the convent," she says.
"I look after an old nun, and I go up every night,
sit with her and make sure she goes to bed."
And I says, "Augh..."
She says, "She's lovely," she says.
"Y'know this, May," she says,
"she's just like your granny -
not the grannies they have now,
but the grannies we knew."
You know these glamorous grannies
that look younger than the mothers some of them...'

Granny Reilly's Wee Shop

'Do you remember Granny Reilly's wee shop?
The choir boys in the Cathedral used to go in
for wine gums, you know, on a practice night.
Now - and this is only a story,
I'd have no proof if it's true -
this night
there were four or five of them went in
and Granny Reilly
had a wee thing she used to stand on
to reach up for the jars of wine gums
and she brought down the jar of wine gums.
"A penn'wo'th a'wine gums,"
and the second wee boy,
"A penn'wo'th a'wine gums."
And she says to the third wee boy,
"A'suppose you want a penn'wo'th a'wine gums too?"
He says, "Naw, a'do not."
She stood up on the wee thing
and put the jar up and she says,
"What *do* you want?"
"I want a hap'wo'th...."'

        'We used to come in
    whenever we came out of the Brownies
for a plate of peas. She used to boil a big pot of peas -
    and they were lovely, and vinegar on them.
      And a penny for a plate of peas,
or you could have got a small saucer of peas,
       was a half p. - a half pence -
    and the big plate for a penny.
And you used to stand in the shop and eat the peas,
     and dear, they were lovely.
    She used to leave the vinegar,
      "There now, love..."
and an oul', oul' woman she was.'
'God, she was a quare age.'
     'And she was dressed in the long black..'
'Aye, in the long dress, and the shawl...'
      'And she had this wee shop.'
'And the wee shawl round her.'
     'And they all called her Granny Reilly.'
'Aye, Reilly was her name.'

'You see she reared her grand-daughter.
She went out to Canada.
She reared the grand-daughter, you see,
and she always called her "granny".
Then everyone else called her granny too.'
'She used to ask you to keep her the papers,
and she'd give you a penny for the week's papers
for putting sweets in.'
'And the minute you would have come round the door,
"A'hope you 'ave the right money,"
before you asked what you wanted,
"A' hope you're not lookin' for change...
hope you've the right money."'
'In for your brandy balls.'

'She used to be a great turn...
"There, now, a'put three in extra
for Christmas for ya," she used to say.
I remember that as well...'

16

Cowboys and Onions

'Sometimes my Aunt May
would have come over to sleep with us too -
an odd time Aunt May would have come over, and -
I think you must have gone into the back room...'

                                        'Aye.'

'She was put into the back room.
She was in with Mammy and Daddy.'

                        'I just remember the bed.
                        It's funny , I can as clear,
                        I can hear my Mammy saying,
                            "C'mon in here, love."
                        They would have fought with me,
                        or I would have fought with them.
                    I suppose I was getting on their nerves,
            And my mother used to say, "C'mon you in here love,"
                    and I just would have been ploughing in
                            behind her and my daddy
                    and getting away down, and it was great.'
'And my Aunt May was wild about onions,
and she used to say,
"Who's going to go down and peel the onion the night?
Whose turn was it last night?"
and she would have gone down, got an onion,
and cut it up...'

                        'Good for your chest.'

'Say nothing, say nothing!
And she would have cut up the onion
and a drop a salt on it, and brought it up.
And we'd have been all sitting in the bed
eating this raw onion.
It was lovely.'

                        'And then we'd have said,
                        "Now, we're going to sing.
                What are you going to sing? C'mon Harry."
                            And the light was out,
                            and this was in the dark.
                        So Violet, Aunt May and myself
                        were in one of the big double beds
                        and Jim and Harry were in the other,
                    and she was in with Mammy and Daddy.
                                So you would say,
                "Go on...what are y'going to sing the night, Jim?"

'Well Jimmy only knew the one song,
I think it was *Cowboy*.
So he would have said, "Augh, well,
augh I don't want to sing..."
"Augh c'mon Jim...hurry up and get started!"
So he would have said, "All right,
I'll sing *Cowboy*."
So he would have sung,
"Cowboy -you're a real humdinger,
you're a hillybilly singer,
you're a *cowboy*..."
And we'd have been under the clothes nearly afraid to laugh.
And then Harry -
he was a different kind of singer altogether...'
                              'Ah gosh, them were the days.'
'They were great days. We were all very close.
I think that's why the families were far closer then,
I do indeed.
And it didn't do any of us any harm,
the five of us sleeping in the one room.'
              'And that's the way it was in every house, but.'
'Every house had two bedrooms,
no matter how many family there were.'
                        'And there was families far bigger than us...'

The Gulley Man

'In fact
they had a whole lot
of characters.'

                              'Indeed they had.'
'They really had characters.'

                              'There was Will
                              - William was one.
                              And he was a big old man -
                              everybody was afraid of him -
                              and he wore a hard hat.'

'Always
wore a hard hat.'

                              'And a black suit
                              and a big rose
                              in his buttonhole.'

'And we were all afraid of him.
But I was terrified
of the Gulley Man.
There is no Gulley Man now -
that's a man who came round
to clean the gratings in the street.
Well, you know how the Housing Executive
or whoever
does it now
- this big lorry -
we had a man to do it
and he had a great big thing
with a hook
and he lifted off the grating
and he cleaned out the gratings.
There were three gratings
in our street,
and as soon -
the word
used to go round The Fountain like
- she could tell you -'

                              '"The Gulley Man!"'

'"The Gulley Man!"
- there wasn't a youngster in sight -
it was like a ghost town.
And we all ran into the houses
and closed the door,

19

because,
many a time
my mother used to say to me,
"I'll get -
there's the Gulley Man!".
We were terrified of The Gulley Man
- I didn't know his name.
I just knew him as the Gulley Man.
And one of the gratings in our street
- there was one at the far end,
and I looked in -
our street was a cul de sac,
a dead end,
and there was one grating
in the middle -
it was just outside our room window -
and I used to go,
slip into the room
and get in behind the curtain,
and I looked-out the step,
and as soon as he came up
and stopped at our step,
I put the curtain back.
And then I'd watch again.
And he finished that grating.
And I used to go out
and stand in the hall
behind the front door
- in those days the door was easy -
and as soon
as he'd gone round the corner,
fifteen minutes
after he'd left The Fountain,
all the doors opened - every article.
That's true.'

                                                'That's true.'

'Terrified -
we were terrified of
the Gulley Man.
I remember my wee girl there.
She was only about two
or three
or something like that.
I remember taking her up one day
- her father had her in his arms.
I saw the Man
- the Gulley Man as he was known -

20

and I said to my husband, Bertie,
I said,
'Oh, there's the Gulley Man!'
And we stopped.
Well, she was terrified,
and she put her head away in here,
and she was joukin' out
to see if this Gulley Man
was away yet.
That was another character
was around,
and,
wait till we see,
who else was there, now..'

The Ben Weed Race

'You believed some of these stories, you see.
They used to always tell you stories
on Hallowe'en Night.
And I, at one time,
I had my arm tied to my brother
with thread,
my eldest brother,   .
and salt threw over my shoulder -
I wouldn't go to sleep
until this was done,
"You'll be goin' wi' the Ben Weeds the night,
you're the right size!"
I was small, you see.'

> 'You threw all the salt
> over your shoulder
> to keep the devil away.'

'Just a pinch, you know.
You just did that there,
and then I had to tie my arm with thread,
black thread,
because this was the superstition, you see,
that kept you from what they called
The Ben Weeds Race,
for Hallowe'en.
It was all wee, small people
and they would name such and such a one
was taking part,
"And, now, you'll have to be there,"
and I was that frightened
I tied myself to my big brother.
You had to be wee, just, small.
And that scared the wits out of you.
I believed that, I did.'

> 'You believed
> in all them oul' things then,
> you see,
> there were no doctors...'

'Boys used to be reading
and they'd say to you,
"Are you taking part in the Ben Weed Race?
I'll see you the night!"
That used to be the crack...'

Aisling

'My mother's best friends,
they lived at our corner,
down right on Bishop Street corner
and they were Catholics.
They were the Breslins,
and the mother visited our house
up till my mother died.
Every week
she came up to see my mother.
And the woman next door,
she was one of these good living women,
she was a Baptist,
and she was a lovely singer.
And Lily McLaughlin used to say,
"Go and send in for Jinny to come in
till she sings."
And she would come in
and Lily would say,
"Go on and sing us *The Old Rugged Cross*,
I love that."
And we would have been singing
all the wee hymns,
Jinny Taylor and my mother
and Lily McLaughlin and me,
and there was no talk about religion.'

                       'You never thought...'

'I remember one night
they came to burn Tommy Martin out,
and the thing that I couldn't understand
- why Tommy Martin?
Why not Powers's,
Kelly's or Danny Grant?
Why Tommy Martin?
And Kathleen Simpson and me
sat on his step
until two in the morning,
guarding,
not to let them in.
They were going to put things in the letter box
and we sat on his step.
Tommy never forgot that to us.
Says I,

24

"If you burn him
you'll burn us along with him.
What did Tommy Martin ever do on you
or any one on this street?"'

                'And Tommy Martin lived in the house
                        just facing hers.'

'And he had one daughter,
Aisling,
and my friend that I ran about with
reared her,
because the both of them worked in the pub.
And she,
Margaret,
was a dress fitter,
and Margaret was out.
And then she worked in the pub
at night,
and Aisling and Kathleen

25

were in my house
nearly every day
and we were the best of friends.
And whenever Tommy got his compensation
he moved down to Bridge End.

'They bought an hotel,
and we were all invited down
to the opening,
when it opened.
And when Aisling went down to live there
she wouldn't take the Free State butter.
She said she wanted the butter
with the Red Hand.
It was just because she was used
with this butter with the Red Hand.
And then at the end up,
she went off butter completely.
Now she's away in America
coming out to be a lawyer
or something.

'Tommy waited till his pub was built
down in the South,
and he used to say
that Aisling
was the only one
that could sing *The Soldier's Song*
in The Fountain
and *The Sash* -
she sang *The Sash* to them
one night down in the South - y'know.
There was a party on
and they were all makin' of her
because she was the owner's daughter
and they asked her
to sing them a song
and she sang *The Sash*.
And Tommy says she's the only one
could sing *The Sash*
down there
and *The Soldier's Song*
in The Fountain.
But she was only five year old or so,
or six.
He says she could do it.
Nobody would have said anything till her.'

The Menu

'We had very good food...'
　　　　　　　　　　　　　　　　'It was all plain food,
　　　　　　　　　　　　　　　　　　　　no pizzas,
　　　　　　　　there was no pizzas or burgers or all these things.
　　　　　　　　　　　　　　　　Everybody in The Fountain,
　　　　　　or everybody, I think, in Derry, had the same menu.
　　　　　　　　　There was one day a week there was stew,
　　　　　there was one day a week there was bacon and turnips,
　　　　　there was one day a week there was mince and onions,
　　　　　and in the warm weather there was a big dish of rice.'
'Rice - God, the rice was lovely...'
　　　　　　　　　　　　　　　　　　　　　　　'Soup.'

'Soup.
Everybody made a pot of soup on a Saturday night,
so, that's the sort of thing...'
　　　　　　　　　　　　　　'And everybody had the same.
　　And Friday night tea you went to the fish and chip shop.'
'And there was always a big fry up on a Sunday morning.'
　　　　　　　　　　　　　　　　　　　　'That's right.'
'Everything in the house was fried -
bacon, eggs, sausage, black pudding, soda bread,
everything.'
　　　　　　'And you had a great dinner on a Sunday always,
　　　　　　　　and a pudding after your dinner on a Sunday.'
'Only once a week.'
　　　　　　　　'None through the week, but on a Sunday.'
'You had a gas cooker.
The gas was on the mains then,
not the bottle gas - the mains gas.
They took away the gas there a couple of years ago
- it used to be down Stanley's Walk.
There was always a wild smell -
not in the houses -
but if you went down around the gas yard. Well...'
　　　　　　　　　　　　　　'You cut the bread yourself.'
'And it was beautiful bread.'
　　　　　　　　　　　　　　　　'Aw, it was lovely.'
'And the breadman.'
　　　　　　　'There were no supermarkets, you see,
　　　　　so there were always what you call breadmen.
　　　　　　　　　　　They delivered the bread.'
'My father was a breadman.'

'And everybody had their own breadman,
and you'd have gone out
and he'd the loaves on shelves
and he'd have big drawers
with the cookies and the buns and the tarts,
and you just went out and picked what you wanted.
There was some sliced bread, but it was mostly unsliced,
you sliced your own.'
'But there weren't any supermarkets, you see,
it was just wee...'

'...small shops, corner shops...'
'...wee small shops.
And you had milkmen
coming in from the country with a van -
with a cart.
And he would have had big churns of milk...'

'Victor.'

'...and buttermilk,
and people would have gone out with their jugs
and took the milk out of the churn,
and he always brought in country butter
and went round the doors selling fresh eggs.
It was all good, fresh food - all fresh -
fresh vegetables and all...'

The Cooks

'Compositions?
I was never any good at compositions -
no imagination...'
                            'Reading, Writing and Arithmetic -
                                there was no Science.
                    We did Reading, Writing, Arithmetic,
                            History, Geography, Algebra.'
'Ah, Algebra was a mystery,
a complete mystery to me.'
                            'But we didn't do that up until
                the year before - two years before we left school -
                    we did Algebra and Geometry, Sewing and...'
'We started off in babies' class
and then first, second, third,
fourth and fifth, sixth and seventh...'
                            'Seventh was the last class.
            And they did Algebra and Geometry in those classes
                        but they didn't do them in the other ones,
                    and we did Reading, Writing and Arithmetic,
                        History, Geography, Sewing and Knitting
                            and - you call it - Home Economics
                        - Cookery - we would just have called it
                                                    Cookery.'
'We did it at the Tech.
We had to go away down to the Tech to do it
from school.
They had no facilities,
no kitchens at all in the schools.
Tuesday we went,
and we used to go every Tuesday
down to the Tech -
the Technical College down in the Strand -
we used to go down there from half ten to half twelve.'
                            'The things we made you couldn't eat,
                but nevertheless you got out of school for two hours.
                        Even my brother wouldn't eat them,
                            and that was saying something.'
'When we were going to school it was in the war
and the stuff was very hard to get
because everything was rationed,
and we had to take sugar if we were making apple tarts,
we had to take sugar and apples

and we had to take margarine,
well, even the margarine was all rationed.'
                    'Flour and all these things were all rationed.
                              It was very hard to get the stuff.
        It was hard because sometimes we only had to take one
                                                    spoonful -
                            it was all written down -
        one level spoonful of cream of tartar or baking powder -
                    which meant we had to buy a whole tin
                                to get a wee thimble...'
'Or if your mother wasn't a baker -
if she was a baker she would have all this stuff in,
but,
and even then, with it being during the war
and all the stuff rationed, you know,
we didn't have all that much stuff.
People would just go on from week to week, you know,
till they got their ration the next week.
And you had a ration book,
and it was marked off in your ration book.'
                    'You were only allowed so much butter
                              to do you for a week.'
'And so much sugar...'
                                        'Bacon, now...'

The Bannister

'I was always getting a thump.
In the Cathedral School, now,
there's a bannister -
it's still there -
and it comes down in a curve.
Well, my friend and me,
we just came out, over went the leg
and down this bannister.'

                    'Sliding down the bannister.'

'And at the foot of the banister was
the Low McCauley
waiting on us with a big stick
for being *un*ladylike -
she was going to learn us to be ladylike -
and now, funny, I had a letter
from a friend of mine that was at school with me
and they emigrated to Canada,
and she writes to me yet
and she wanted to know
"was the old Cathedral bannister
that we used to slide down still there?"
and I said that it was - still there -
and many a good thump we got over the head of it.
And one thing that I remember about The Fountain
on Patrick's Day, well there was an old saying
that that was the day the stone turned,
and a lady said to me, "Why do you say the stone turned?"
I says, "I just don't know,
but they say the stone turned on Patrick's Day -
the next day was the beginning of Summer.
So my mother got us all ready for a picnic.
We were off school for Patrick's Day
and we went out to a place called The Bolies,
and we lit a wee fire,
and my mother had boiled eggs for us
and different things, to have a picnic.
So she always warned us going out,
"Look," she says, "I'm letting you go now,
and I'm depending on you.
Now," she says, "I don't want you to stay out too long,
for I would be worried about you" -
we were home for our dinner - we had everything ate.'

The Deanery School

'The Deanery School -
there was a man they called Armstrong
was the headmaster in my day
and we had a master there called Humpy...
I forget his name...
and there was a man they called Ankatel -
two junior masters and the headmaster -
and the school was girls and boys,
but it wasn't mixed -
the playground even was separate.
There was a big sliding door between the two.
It was only on a special occasion
that the whole school would have met.
There was Sarah McCauley and Jane McCauley
and a Miss Irvine - you know Irvine's the printers? -
his sister was a teacher there -
and there was a wee woman they called Mooney,
Miss Mooney.
I always thought Miss Mooney was an angel.
She was the greatest wee soul at all.
We used to go out and deliberately bump our head -
get a big bump on your head -
went over to Miss Mooney and she gave you a penny
to hold on it -
and a penny in them days was money -
and then when you got the bump a-sort-of down
you went over to Miss Mooney
to give her back the penny,
"Oh just keep it!" Well!
I often wonder I wasn't addle-brained -
it was all part of the scheme in them days.
She was in the infants' class.
Now in the infants' class in those days
there was a kind of platform -
there were steps, actually, as if they were steps,
extended from one side of the room
to the other,
and these were terraced,
and that's where we were taught.
And you had a slate
and another bit of slate for writing with.
There were no notebooks in those days.'

The Deanery Excursion

'And we had the Deanery Excursion
and it was always the name,
'The Deanery'
and 'The Deanery Schools',
we knew it
when we went there,
yet the actual name of it
is the 'Cathedral School',
I never knew why.
We would have went up there
on the morning of the excursion -
we never slept a wink the night before,
afraid of our lives
we would miss the train.
We went down to the Buncrana train,
and we got the Buncrana train.
We marched down there,
and we had all wee flags with us.
With that, the Deanery Band,

which was a flute band
made up out of the locals
of The Fountain,
they played us down.
Away before that
there was the wee band
they started up there,
The Maiden City Band.
A man they called...
between Bobby Jackson
and Johnny Reeves,
they started it up.
They would have played us down
to the Swilly station -
Lough Swilly station -
and we boarded the train there for Buncrana.
Got down there
and we would have run around,
then about twelve o'clock
we got refreshments,
which was a cup of tea and a bag of buns,
assorted buns -
more like baps than buns -
no pastry in those days,
and we enjoyed ourselves -
there were sports -
wee prizes for that,
and we got tea
about four o'clock in the evening
and about six o'clock
back on to the train again for home -
a thoroughly enjoyable day.
The Dean and all
was there
the Sunday School teachers and all
were there,
making sure you didn't get into any devilment -
there were maybe a couple of hundred of us.
That was Dean King...'

Mr Beattie

'There was no money for education -
I never remember being well off,
never -
we lived
and that was just it.
Only I got my scholarship
for the North West College
I would never have been able to go...
Mr Beattie -
he was called Sheriff Beattie -
and we loved Mr Beattie.
There was Mr Beattie,
Mr Berry, Mr Sullivan,
Miss Guthrie, Miss Thompson
and Miss Irvine
and it was a very, very happy school.
And we played up on the wall -
that was the keep-fit
was on the wall,
and there was a small railing
round the Cathedral
at the bottom
and that was the playground
for the small ones.
And my best friend
at the North West College
was Teresa McAnulty,
and Myra Connor and I
got very, very friendly,
and she bought me my wedding cake -
and you had to ask a dispensation
from the priest
to attend the wedding,
because in those days they didn't attend
each other's wedding,
so at the last minute
she was able to come and say to me,
"I'm allowed to come to your wedding" -
and she bought me my wedding cake.'

Singing School

'The only thing I couldn't do,
which, as it turned out I was quite happy I couldn't do,
was,
I couldn't sing.
And, you see, the Cathedral was a great singing school
for the reason that all the boys were in the choir,
and that meant that you had to go about four days a week
up to choir to practice,
and then on Sunday
you had to go about three times on a Sunday,
and I was a kind of a soccer fanatic
and it suited me down to the ground that I didn't have to sing.
The only sport was the soccer - there was no rugby -
rugby would have been a gentleman's game at that time.
They had a team called the Corinthians,
and they won the Irish Junior Cup, which was a big thing.
In nineteen-twenty-one they won the Irish Junior Cup.
That would have been All Ireland at that particular time.
They were a good team.
They were the second Derry team to do it.
The first team was nineteen-ten, Derry Guilds won it.
There are only three or four Derry teams that have won it
down the years.
And all Fountain teams after that
were called either The Corinthians or The Casuals.
The Corinthians were the famous English amateur team -
They were all public schoolboys,
and their second eleven was known as Casuals.
It was away back in nineteen-ten or nineteen-eleven they
were formed.
I remember my father telling a tale about it
that they played a final at Coleraine
and there was an old chap in The Fountain, Ben Rutledge -
I remember he was a very stout man with a moustache,
and he was a bit of an enterpre-te-neur,
and he went over to the station
to get a train to Coleraine for the match
and the station wouldn't put on a train for the match,
so he hired a train,
and he made a lot of money -
he was supposed to have made a lot of money -
and after that the railways would never hire a train again...'

Dances

'Listen, see the girls now,
they haven't the same picking as we had...'
'When the boats came down...'
'...the ships used to be tied up from the bridge...'
'Aye, from the bridge right down.
Bobby Frazer used to be tortured
- no - Bobby was away then himself.
But they used to be tortured
"When's the boats coming in?"'
'They called The Memorial Hall the 'Naval Hall' then.'
'The American Navy
took over the Memorial Hall during the war
and they used to have dances in it.
And we never got white bread, you see,
then,
during the war.
But whenever the Americans were there,
when they had a dance,
they used to have sandwiches maybe
- white bread -
and if any sailor took an interest in you that night,
you got round him and said,
"Wonder could you get us some of them sandwiches
to take home to me mother?"
And they would have gone and made up a parcel
of white...
God it was great
to be taking home a parcel
of white bread sandwiches!'
'They had it when we hadn't...'
'You see the Americans got all their stuff.'
'For our eggs and all were rationed.'
'There was nothing, you see, we had nothing.'
'I didn't like the Yanks.
I never bothered.'
'No, and I didn't either. I never liked the Yanks,
but the Yanks had the dances.
We used to go to the dances in the Memorial Hall
when they had a big dance,
because they always had a big band there.
It used to be great.'
'When the Yanks came here at first

they thought they were superior to everybody else.
They thought you were nobody,
and it was a privilege to be seen with them.
And one date and they wanted you to go to bed -
that's why I never liked them.'
                              'Sure they always said
                        if there'd a been another war
              they would only have had to send the ammunition
                                    for the Yanks left
                    enough sons here to fight the next war.'
'That's honest to God.'
                        'They did surely to goodness.
                Nearly every other girl had a young -
          not a son - for some of them had daughters.'
'Sure there was always the joke
that every time a house,
a furnished house,
was taken by Yanks,
all us young fellas used to stand outside
watching the carry-on at night time.
They never pulled curtains
nor blinds or anything,
just straight up the stairs and into bed...'
                              'The next war
                  they'll not have to send the troops
          for they've already left them behind them -
                                    sons...'
'But there were sailors billeted in The Fountain.'
                        'Sailors, that's right,
                  and we got on great with them.'
'But when you went to a dance
the fellas that were left...'
                              'The civvies...'

'...they would have been saying,
"It's a waste of time going the night -
the boats are in -
they'll not look at us the night."
They were raging
because the girls all went with the sailors
to get cigarettes and all off them.
But the civvies would have said,
"What are we going the night for, sure..."
and then when the boats went out,
the civvies all came in after us and said,
"Aye, look at them all the night -
they're all round us the night
and there are no sailors."'

Drawing the Line

'Aw, we had good fun.
Well, when you had no money to go anywhere...
But, at the weekend you went to the pictures,
and sometimes during the week.
I was very lucky,
because I had an old woman sat beside me in the factory,
and she had no family
and she more or less took me on as her daughter,
and she used to say,
"Are you goin' out the night, Lily?"
and I'd say, "Naw, I have no money,"
It was only thru'pence then to get into a dance -
and she'd say,
"There's thru'pence, go on to the dance the night,"
and I would have been away over to the Victoria Hall,
the 'Towers Ballroom' as they called it,
and that was a great night for thru'pence...'
                    'And I used to come in on the bicycles...'
'When it come to a dance...'
                                        'I came in.'
'...she got the strength.'
            'There was a woman out the Brae, a Miss Fletcher,
                    and she used to keep our bicycles,
            and if it was a wet night we'd come in in wellingtons
                    and she'd have kept our wellingtons
                till we came out of the dance, because -
the mucky roads, you see, you would have been all muck -
        and then she kept our wellingtons and our raincoats
            and then we would have walked out to the Legion
                                or the Towers,
                whichever dance we were going to.'
'I wore high heels from I left school.
Stilletto heels came in in the fifties,
and the worst thing that ever happened -
that's what left me a cripple the day.'
                    'We didn't feel it hard to walk in.
    I would have walked miles, if I was going to a dance.
                I even went to a dance one night
                    with a pair of my sister's shoes,
            and she wore a size smaller than me -
and I couldn't even dance the whole night - I had to sit.
        And above all nights - not that I ever got rushed -

39

> but above all nights
> I got asked more times than enough,
> and I had to let on I had a sore foot -
> so I had -
> My two big toes were bent like that, look...'

'And The New Look -
do you see that style - the long skirts, buttoned up.
Well that was the style, you know.
It was all straight skirts,
and I remember having a blouse,
a gypsy blouse - off the shoulders. -
I remember that as well.'

> 'And you tanned your legs -
> you bought stuff in the chemist
> and put it on your legs - that was during the war.
> And if you were any way artistic,
> you drew a line up the back
> to let on you had stockings on you.'

'But I never drew the line.'

> 'No, neither did I.'

'And then if you went to a dance with it raining
when you arrived...'

> 'Your legs!'

'...your legs were all starred at the front.'

40

The Bars

'And I remember on the back of every toilet door
there was a notice and it said,
"THESE LAVATORIES ARE YOURS.
THEY ARE, WE ARE TOLD,
THE FINEST IN NORTHERN IRELAND.
IT IS IN YOUR OWN INTEREST
THAT YOU KEEP THEM IN PERFECT CONDITION".
And that was behind every toilet door.
And we went there to smoke -
because we had nowhere else to go -
and you weren't allowed to smoke. Now, years ago,
the girls could smoke where they worked, you know,
they used to light the cigarette and have a puff
and leave it down beside them.
In the smaller factories they did that
but you weren't allowed down here.
Violet told me that.'
                            'Aye, but that was years before that again.'
'I remember there was one day
there were no chairs in the toilet
so we sat on our hunkers on the floor
and, you know, when you stand all day you
just love a seat to get sitting down.
Most of the girls that worked on machines
liked to stand for five minutes,
but we were always desperate to get sitting down,
so we would go into the toilet, two of us,
and one would sit this way, and the other that way.
So we were sitting having a grand smoke.
And one day there was two girls in the next toilet,
and they didn't know that we'd come in,
and they were telling all the bars about the night before.
And Ella says to me, "Shhh.."
and we were listening and it was great
and just as it got to the last exciting bit what do you think?
Somebody went in to that toilet and pulled the chain
and we never heard the end of the story.
Well, the girl I worked with, Ella, was very quick.
An' she started - very quick-tempered -
"If I get that so-an'-so that pulled that chain!"
And we never heard the end of that story, now...
whether her and him finished or not...'

Gossamer

'Mine is not interesting at all -
the Memorial Hall
wasn't it, Tommy?'

       'Aye, the Memorial Hall.'

'Tommy was from The Fountain,
and we met
and we were standing talking.'

       'She was the interloper.'

'I was the interloper,
and I just met him.
We were all coming home
in a crowd.
We didn't go together.
We were always in a crowd,
Iris Kitson and all them,
and - do you mind Lila Burton?
Lila - me and her had fallen out or something,
and Iris Kitson says to me,
"Let on you're w'Tommy..."and I -
who was the fella was with you?'

       'Sam Barr, wasn't it?'

'I let on that we were together,
you know, to Lila Burton.
And then that was the start of it
there.'

     'She started then going with him,
          God help him.'

'It started
the night we walked in to the big dance -
the Fire Brigade dance
in Castlederg -
and the cobwebs smothered us.'

      'Aye, the big dance -
      we all went in the bus,
     and we went up the hall
    and the cobwebs were hanging.'

'As soon as you stepped in the door -
the cobwebs -
I never forgot that.'

       'Aye, that was the -
      what do you call that
     that the fairies, the angels?'

'Gossamer.'

'Aye, that's what it was.'

'And I worked all my life
in the factory.
And when you got married
they put you in a hamper on wheels
and they tied your coat up
with a hundred strings.
They tied your hair up
and threw old shoes after you.
About four or five girls
put strings up your sleeves,
up the sleeves of your coat.
They tied up your coat,
your whole coat and then -
that was the last thing they did
they fired the coat after you then
on your way out.'

'There was a girl worked with me,
what's this you called her?
She lived away down at
Fahan -
down in the Free State -
and they took her..
She went to run out
and they took her into a cloakroom
and there were big central heating pipes
with, you know,
big screws up on them
like that.
And they held her down and
they forgot about this thing on her back.
And whenever they let her go
she couldn't move,
and they had to phone the ambulance
to take her to hospital.
And she was in the hospital -
nearly missed her wedding -
she was in the hospital
for nine days.
And do you see to this day,
Maureen -
what's this they called her -
she's wild with her back
to this day.
And it was the girls
pressing down on her.'

44

Fate

'There was a bone fire
up in a wee street
off The Fountain,
and I went up
to see the bone fire -
I went to have a look,
and I leaned over,
and didn't somebody throw a squib
into it,
and it sparked,
and I jumped,
and I jumped into the arms
of the man I married.

But I couldn't even get talking to him -
my brother came up,
"My father says come on down".
I said,
"I'll be down
in a wee minute..."
"My father says
if you don't come down
he'll come up for you now!"
So I had to go down.

But I met him again anyway.
I was in the hospital,
I had a big operation,
and my grand-daughter was in
visiting.

And this lady came over to me
and she asked me
how I was keeping and all,
and she turned round
to my grand-daughter
and she says to her,
"You know,
I could have been your..."
she was very polite,
"...I could have been your

grandmama, "
she said.
"I had a very big notion of your granda
when he was young."
And my grand-daughter says to her,
"Well
could I ask you -
how many of a family you have now?"
She says, "Three."
And my grand-daughter says,
"Well you were lucky -
for she has eight!"
I was fifty-two years married to him
when he died.
My grand-daughters always say to me,
when I go to the doctor's,
"No fun!"
But I had to go to -
what do you call
the coloured doctor
up in Altnagelvin?'

           'Augh, I don't know -
           there are that many ...'

'I forget his name,
but he said
he was finished with me
and shook hands,
and I said to him,
"Well, thank you very much, doctor,
but, " says I,
"You never got me a man."
"But," says I -
the grand-daughter was standing -
"Thees'uns
would object".
"Excuse me," he says,
"could I ask you something?
Who, or what,
are *thees'uns*?"
My grand-daughter says,
"We're *thees'uns*,
and it's 'these ones'
that's Irish she's coming out with" -
He didn't know
what
I was talking about.'

Big Nights

'...all the old songs.'

'All the old songs.'

'Only A Beautiful Picture.'

'A beautiful picture.'

'You know that
"a beautiful picture
in a beautiful golden frame"
and *The Ring Your Mother Wore*
and *The Midnight Express...'*

'There's A Long, Long Trail A'Winding.'

'You know all these old songs,
but they were a treat to listen to. -
I'm talking about my own mother, but..'

'She has every right, in my book,
to boost
about her mother singing
for her mother
had a beautiful voice
and whenever there was a wedding
there were big nights...'

'In the houses, you know.'

'Before the girl got married,
and even when a fellow got married,
all the neighbours and everything
gathered in
but especially when the girls
were getting married
you gathered in the house.
You maybe had three big nights.'

'You would have had a night
for the relatives
and a night for neighbours
and a night for the girls..'

'And a night for the girl's work friends,
mates you know.'

'And my mother and Aunt Lizzie
were invited to all these.'

'And there was the tea.'

'Augh, tea?
Talk about tea?
All fresh, all home baked stuff.'

'Everybody helping.'

'Everybody helped.
It was all home baked stuff.'

      'And chairs carted in
        from other houses.'

'And the crockery was lent
and you all gathered in.'

      'Everybody had a sort-of-a
        party piece, you know...'

'When I could sing I sang.
I learnt all the old songs
that my mammy knew.
My mammy had a lovely voice.'

      'I would have sung
        more,
      a wee bit more modern,
but I hated singing in front of people.
How we ever got up in Butlin's and sang
I'll never know...'

The Bride Boat

'Now there was a young girl in The Fountain
married a Yank -
and she was beautiful
and so was he.
The two of them,
they were two visions.
If you had seen them.
And do you know,
now they're retired
and they're back living in Portstewart
They retired back here
and they're living in Portstewart now.'

           'Who was that?'

'Now I don't know what her married name is.
The father, her father and mother
went out to America.
She went out in the boat.
Do you remember they took -
what is this they called it? The Bride...'

           'The Bride Boat.'

'The Brides' Boat from...'

           'Lisahally.'

'Lisahally.
It sailed out from Lisahally
and took all the brides out to America,
and she went out on that.
And then her mother and father went out to America
to live.
They emigrated out there,
and I think they're both dead now.
But this girl,
her family's still out there.
I think she had a son and daughter.
And she and her husband retired to Portrush,
or Portstewart, now.
But she was a lovely girl,
and so was he...'

        'And there were some Derry girls married Yanks,
and whenever they went out,
although the Yankee...'

'They got suckie-ins...'

           'Suckie-ins...'

'Although the Yank looked white,
whenever they went out
their mother-in-laws were negroes.
That happened to two or three.'

                              'I remember them
                    standing outside Welch's one morning.
                              We were waiting to get in
                              and they were saying,
                    "Dear, did y'hear about so-and-so
                    she got word from her daughter
                    and whenever she went out
                    his family was all there to meet her
                    and the mother was a negro...'
'But some of them done very well, mind you...'
                              'Oh dear aye.'

'I remember one wee girl.
She lived down the Long Tower,
and she come from a very poor home.
But she married this Yank
and he took her out -
and the photos that she sent back -
with her standing beside the car
and sitting out in the garden,
and a lovely house
and the style of her.'

                    'And I remember the mother coming up
                    to show my mother the photos that she got.
                              She did very well, and,
                                        dear help,
                              she was a lovely wee girl,
                              but she never had clothes.
                              She never was dressed.'

'He met her one night on the Wall.
Her and a crowd were looking over
down into the Guildhall Square
and these sailors saw them,
and they came up.
And this one asked her to go to the pictures
and she said, " Ah no, I couldn't,"
and one of the other girls said, " Aye,
because she has no shoes."
And he said, "Oh, don't you worry about that,"
he said,
"I don't care what way you're dressed."
And he just fell for her,
and he took that wee girl just the way she was,
and she did very well...'

The War

'I joined up with the Territorials on the fourth of April 1939
and we were called up to service in September 1939.
We were kept at home here for about a month or so.
We were moved away in November.
They put us on board trains
and we went right through France down to Marseilles
and we got the ship down there,
the *Etterick*,
for Egypt.
We landed in Egypt round about the end of November.
Then we went down through the Sudan,
down to Aden.
I do remember, on one occasion,
there was a fellow -
we were in Port Sudan.
We went up with McLean,
he was an officer, a captain,
and coming down again we saw this figure coming along.
And he says to me, "Who in under goodness is that?"
He was coming along with his full pack and all.
I says, "I don't know till I get down his length
to see if I know him".
And when we got down the length of him
I recognised him.
Of course the captain says, "Stand man!"
He says to him, "Where are you going, man?"
He says, "I'm goin' home,
I've had enough of this carry on!"
He says, "Get on man!"
That regiment, Twenty-four, Twenty-five Battery
were all Derry men, part Strabane, Limavady -
land's sakes alive,
when we left there must have been
a thousand left the City.
The first one we lost
was a fellow called Tommy Porter -
shrapnel in the stomach -
poor Tommy,
he was an inoffensive fellow.
It killed him in no time at all.
Jim Gilmore was killed in Italy
when the bomb went into the gun-pit. '

Aleppo

'I was transferred to the Royal Engineers
and I went up
into the Lebanon and Syria
and up as far as the Turkish border.
And there was a place
they called Aleppo.
That's where the train came in
from Turkey
and that's where the spies came in.
It was no uncommon sight
to see one of these boys
trailed out and...
that was the last you seen of them.
And I know that they had a special car.
The BSM,
the British Security Mission
were the people responsible
for those people.
Well now,
two or three of these boys, it appears,
had the cyanide pill in the button,
popped it in the mouth,
killed themselves.
So what they did was,
they had this car specially fitted.
When they put them into it
they were handcuffed
to the ceiling,
the roof of the car,
and their ankles,
so they could put nothing in their mouths,
and that was the way they travelled
from that
down to Jerusalem -
that was where their interrogation went on.
There was one fellow I met -
he was a Southern Irishman -
he was Twenty-four British Security Mission
and he told me
if they weren't important
they cross questioned them
there and then.

He says, "And I had the job,"
he says, "of removing them ...
disposing of them" -
and the casual way he said it -
and I said,
"What did you do?"
"Aw, " he says,
"I said to them,
'Down on your knees
and say your prayers -
whatever prayers you have to say,'
and I gave them a burst
of a Thompson sub-machine-gun".
Very callous...
Thank God
I never had to kill anybody myself -
gave them bad enough looks,
but never
had to kill them...'

Sir Basil

'Sir Basil McFarland and him
were like that.
I never got a letter from him that Sir Basil censored
but he put a wee note at the bottom of it for me.
He put a wee note at the bottom for me.
He would just write at the bottom of it,
"Don't worry Margaret,
I'm keeping this man in order -
he'll not get into any harm,
I'm looking after him -
I'm doing fairy godfather to him..."
His father and Sir Basil were great friends.'

'He was the battery commander.
There were a lot of us joined the Territorials,
the TA,
in nineteen thirty nine,
April and that.
In those days they were very, very exacting
when they were giving you a medical.
You were hopping round in the nude
for about an hour.
There was one fellow said to me,
"I had to touch my toes
and they counted the knobs on my spine",
but once the war started
they used to say
you went in to the MO
and he touched you
and if you were warm - A1.
But Sir Basil was a great fellow altogether -
one of the best.
And when we were there
King Farouk and Queen Farida -
she was expecting.
And it became known
that if she had a boy
we would get a medal -
there would be a medal struck
for all the British soldiers -
but she had a wee girl
and all we got
was a packet of fags.'

Getting Religion

'One time in the middle of the desert
when we were lying in camp -
every Sunday morning, roll call, everybody on parade -
now the usual was,
"Right, fall in
RC's there,
Presbyterians there,
Methodists there,
Church of Ireland, England - anything else - there -
heathens over there".
So, I decided I had got fed up with this lark
of marching down to Church Parade every Sunday,
so I fell out with the heathens.
So the Sergeant Major looked at me and he says,
"Well, what's wrong with you?"
"Ah," says I, "I have given up religion, Sir."
"Have you now?" he says.
"Tell you what," he says, "go to the quartermaster's stores."
There was three of us.
"Go to the quartermaster's stores -
tell the Q that I sent you up".
Went up to the quartermaster anyway.
Now it was a quarter of a mile from the officers' mess,
where the officers' mess was,
down to the main gate -
it was a wee tarmac road.
But there was what was known locally as
a campsine of wind -
that's what they called this wind,
the Khamsin -
blew the sand -
and it was blowing it all across the place.
We had to brush that sand off that road.
When we got to the bottom
we had to turn and go back up again
and we were going up and down and down and up,
and the boys gave us the gee-up when they saw us coming -
I was the first,
the right-hand marker the next Sunday morning -
I found my religion -
learnt my lesson...'

Alamein

'I was at Alamein.
I was with the Derry regiment.
We were with the Royal Artillery.
We were territorials.
You went over for a month for training every year.'

> 'To England.'

'And, like the boy beside me said,
we needed six months intensive training every year,
and Sir Basil McFarland was our Commander.
You'd got the choice of going to Bude in Cornwall
or going to Alexandria in Egypt for six months.
He picked six months in the Mediterranean,
but during that blinking six months
Italy came into the war,
and instead of being out six months,
we were out five years.
To bring us home
they would have had to take us round the Cape,
and so we didn't get a home leave

till we ended up in Italy.'
'I'll tell you a thing that happened me
when I came back from the army.
I came to the station in the Waterside
and there were some old ladies.
Now, this is the Gospel truth.
One old lady came up,
and I was drunk at the time, and I sent word to my father.
And he was looking for me
and I came off the train and I had a topi and all on me -
what they call a topi -
you see them there in Africa and India.
You know these films that you see?
I was there with the big hat on -
and that's a topi, what we called topis.
And I said to my father, "Hi Da! Do ya not know me?"
Well, he turned around - I'll tell you the word after.
I'm going to tell you straight out -
"Well, ya sunburned looking hure ye..."
I was as black as your boot.
I was pure black. I was nearly ten years away
and had done a year and a half in England.
I did eleven and a half years.'
'I went up the desert along with him.

We were different. '

'I was heavy guns, he was ack ack.
They were the ones that shot the planes.
Our shells were a hundred pounds in weight.'
'I can't remember now the calibre of them, I'm sorry...'

'Well any shell we fired -
you've seen big guns? - well, you've seen a photo of big
guns? - well I've seen them as if you were stripping -
you know the way you would strip a banana? -
in four pieces.
That's the way our guns came back from Benghazi.
We were up in Benghazi
and my greatest pal was a wee desert rat
Remember the wee desert rats?'
'Aye, it was like a wee kangaroo.'

'And I carried him in a box.
It got cold at night, you see. They used to come in
and get under your blankets.'
'We slept in tents...'

'We didn't. It was useless putting up a tent.
The only ones that had tents were another regiment,
the Fifteenth Field Regiment.
You had a blanket, and you put the blanket
over your head and that was you.'
'We weren't moving about as much as you.'

'You were defending the planes.
We were moving about a lot.
If Gerry had a pocket -
a pocket meant
that there were four or five guns in one spot,
the big heavy guns -
we were told to match heavy with heavy.
We were the heavy guns,
and maybe at four o'clock in the morning
they'd say 'Go east six miles', or 'Go west',
whatever it was, and you had to get in there
and start bombing like hell to get them out.
And when we got paid we got drunk.
We went down to Alexandria or Pharoah.
If you were waiting on Alamein
you were either in Pharoah or Alexandria
or some place like that.
You had a good time.
I know a fellow, a mate of mine,
that sold a jeep to the Egyptians
for eight hundred ackers, or whatever it was,
to get drink...'

Meeting the Pope

'As for The Fountain -
I came here twenty-seven years ago -
as I told you, I'm a Roman Catholic
and the Pope put me here
as a missionary to The Fountain -
he couldn't have done a better job.
I was in London working as a plasterer.
I come back and I got a house here,
an old house, just - Jim knows it - and I did it up,
and I wouldn't leave The Fountain
for love nor money.
I was offered very, very good money
during the troubles,
when it *was* the troubles, at their height,
to get out of it because I was a Catholic -
I wouldn't leave it.
The people of The Fountain are -
they're not people - they're angels,
for they - during the troubles there -
they stuck a hell of a lot -
do you understand me? - a hell of a lot,
but yet there was a smile on their face.
And I have never, never, never,
been insulted by the people of The Fountain.
I might have been insulted
by the people outside The Fountain,
and called a Fenian so'an'so and all like that,
but it would have been other people -
do you understand me? -
but as for the people of The Fountain,
now, they are the greatest -
we stick together like shite to a blanket -
I've never had a wrong word
with anybody from The Fountain, have you?'
                              'No, and I've many friends
                    who went to the dances is Catholics
                          and I'll meet them in the street
                      and they'll still stop and talk to me,
                               although after the war,
            when I came back from the war, I was with the police
                             up to nineteen seventy-one.
                  And I had the privilege of meeting the Pope

in Italy after the war...'
'And I never met him at all,
and he sent me into...'
'I was in charge of transport and we went into Rome
to find out where they'd be issuing petrol and diesel
and we found the place.
They were in the charge of the Coldstream Guards there,
and we said, "We'll have a look round here
while we're here".
So we went up to the Vatican
and left the motorbikes and went in.
We were looking up at this big painting
and I says, "Isn't that a marvellous painting there?"
I felt a pinch on my arm, looked round
and the priest was standing.
He says, "You're from Derry!"
Says I, "You seem to be from Derry too..."
"I am," says he. "I'm Monsignor MacDaid."
Says I, "Are you any relation to Jack
that has the wee shop at Creggan Cross
beside Saint Eugene?"
"Ah'm his brother," he says.
Says I, "Jack and I always went to the dances
to the Corinthian..."
So he took me up to his quarters
and took me up to the Pope,
and I says, "Now you tell the Pope
that I'm from The Fountain - I'm not a Roman Catholic".
The Pope would talk away in Italian
and he would interpret
and then the Pope reached for a big
pair of Rosary beads
and held them out in front of me
and I whispered to him,
"Did ya not tell him I was from The Fountain...?"
you see.
He says, "I did,
but the Pope says put them in your kit bag -
it'll take you home safe".
I had to take them here in my kit-bag,
and my mother,
a Catholic woman that she got the paper from
down in Bishop Street,
she says, "Mrs Murray would be delighted to get them
from the Pope", so I says,
"Take them down an' give them till her," -
an' that's how I met the Pope...'

Maggie

'A've another one to tell you..
As I told you, I used to go for messages
on a Monday morning - Monday -
I'd go to school on Monday -
half nine on Monday morning,
and I used to go up and tell Master McCloskey,
"I'll not be back the half day",
and he'd ask me, "Why?"
"I have to do messages.
I have to go into the pawn and all for the people -
across there in Union Street".
But I was carrying this parcel every week
for this old woman - oul' Maggie they called her -
and she always wanted a half-a-crown.
Mundies' wine was a half-a-crown then.
And I'd go straight down and ask for it and come back.
But oul' Jimmy Barr that had the pawn down on the Lecky -
remember Jimmy on the Lecky Road? -
he says, "Look, son, what's in this parcel?"

I says, "A pair o' shoes."
"Are ye sure, now, it is?"
"That's what I'm told anyway -
I'm only goin' a message for oul' Maggie..."
He went out and he went over
and he opened up the parcel.
What was in it?
A brick rolled up in brown paper
and parcelled up in a shoe box again.
He says, "Look," he says -
it shows ye how people were good in them days
and how they realised that people needed money -
he says, "Look, son, there's thru'pence -
don't you say to Maggie that I opened that parcel,
an' just you bring it in on Monday
the same as usual."
And he told his two sons,
"There's a parcel
comes from Maggie Ferguson
an' nobody's to open it.
Just give him -
give the youngster -
the money".
It was always half-a-crown.
That's how good the people were,
and still are, in Derry 'till the present day.
They're some of the nicest people
you could ever ask to meet
in Derry.
I've travelled the world.
I've been in India - I served in India
I've been all over:
the Burmah Road -
not the Burmah Road here -
I've been in Burmah,
I've been in India,
I've been in Egypt -
all over -
where fighting was I was,
right?
I was glad to get back to Derry -
I was more than glad,
because the Derry people are...
they're a people of sainthood
and they don't realise it - they are.
I've been to London -
and was glad to get out of it...'

The Flute

'Once, only once,
I ever went out with an American,
and it was just because the girl I went about with
she had met one,
and Elizabeth and the four of us decided -
it was God's clear daylight -
we were going out the road
a walk
a Saturday night -
and, in fact, we were to come back,
to go to the dance,
that's what it was.
We were dandering down the Strand Road,
and I says to Elizabeth,
"Oh, my God, 'Lizabeth,
there's me daddy away down wi' the van !"
He was goin' down to check on his van, you see,
the place he worked - the Rock.
Well I said, "I'm goin' home,
come on home !"
And, like, you could have pulled him through a flute
and he wouldn't have stopped a note -
a big, thin , oh Lord -
you'd have pulled three for a rifle.
I was affronted,
and I says, "Look,
I'm goin' home get rid a'this boy,
I'm goin' to the dance. "
So we walked up to the end of the street -
it was just clear daylight -
and I was saying to him, like,
that I had to go somewhere,
making a whole...
and who came down but my father.
And he just looked at me, and he says,
"Goodnight", and walked over to the house.
And I remember that American fellow,
he says, "Will he *beat* you? Will I go *over*?"
And I says, "No, I'll be all right".
And I went over to the house.
My father, he was standing.
He was just going to have a wash,

and he was
taking all these things out of his pocket,
you know,
And I thought,
"Oh dear God, what...
I'm goin' t'be murdered the night".
And he just looked up
and he says - know what he says?
"Was that the best you could do?"
Well ...
I felt about thon size
I would rather he had thumped me.
And I didn't know where I was standing -
oh, dear - and that was all.
And I never, ever
went out with an American after it.
And that's what he said -
"Is that the best you could do?"
And, like, a nice looking fellow,
but, I'm not joking you,
he was like thon
and I was trying to hide behind him,
but you couldn't have -
for he was like thon... '

Bananas

'I didn't go out with Yanks.
I never went out with Yanks.
But you'd have got a lecture,
"Be you in at such an' a time, watch yourself now..."
But then the Yank would have come up
with a wee parcel under his arm
and that was it -
with maybe tins of ham or something,
something that we couldn't get during the war.'
                                      'Tinned fruit.'

'Tinned fruit.
And then, you see,
the Church asked you
to take them in
on a Sunday, you know,
to take some of the servicemen in.
And I mind we had ones.
One of them was a cook on a ship,
and every time they came in
they always came up.
And there was one, a carpenter,
and at Christmas time -
they would have come in about Christmas -
they brought my wee boy -
he was only a young fella at the time -
the carpenter brought him a beautiful truck he'd made.
If you had seen the stuff,
the wood,
that was in it...real good stuff.
And the cook come up
with a big roast of pork,
and a big cake - a big Christmas cake,
iced and all -
and, you see,
we had nothing like that.
We got nothing like that.
And fruit -
they brought fruit from abroad,
for I mind my wee boy -
they were giving him a banana -
and he wouldn't eat it.
He didn't know what it was...'

Granny and the Customs

'Once my mammy and daddy were married -
my daddy was in the Specials -
and once they were married
my mammy
didn't go back to work again,
for we had a fair-sized house,
and my granny kept lodgers,
so my mammy had a full time occupation
washing, cooking and cleaning
for the lodgers for my granny.
She worked in the factory
and she went
to her work
at eight o'clock in the morning
and didn't come in till
six o'clock at night.
She worked in a place called Solagi's
in Foyle Street.
She was eighty-six when she was working there -
eighty-six.
There was no retirement age.'
                         'No, there was no retirement age.'
'You worked as long as you could...'
                              'And you were glad of it.
                     You were glad to be able to work.'
'You worked as long
as you could.
There was nobody said to you.
If you were capable of the work,
you worked.
My granny was a smashing baker,
ah, she really was - she was
a good baker.
She made patchwork quilts,
she made shirts
for the grandchildren.
Whenever the cloth and stuff was scarce,
whenever you couldn't have got
material,
we went across the border
and smuggled the material across.
And she made the frocks

for all the girls.
Myself and my cousins,
she made the dresses for us.
You see everything was rationed.'

                                        'You needed
                                        the coupons.'

'Even after the war -
for long enough after the war.
Whenever I was married
in nineteen forty-eight
there was still clothing coupons.
The thing was, everybody did it.
It was just a way of life.
Practically everybody in the City
went across the border.
Either you went to
St Johnstown...'

                                        'Bridge End...'

'...or you went to Moville or Muff
or something like that.
Whenever I was working in the factory
I thought nothing,
whenever I finished my work,
of coming home and getting my tea
and meeting three or four girls.
We might have been lucky enough to get
the bus
from The Diamond
to Messines Park,
and you'd get out of the bus at Messines Park
and walk to Bridge End
and walk back again.
You might have missed the bus
and you had to walk then up to The Fountain,
laden.
You had tea, sugar, butter,
sweets, cigarettes.
And you were dodging the patrol cars,
you were dodging the customs men.
And on the winter nights,
whenever there was a heavy frost,
and nights there was snow,
whenever you saw them coming
you were diving
to get into the ditch,
and sometimes you were muck
to the eyes...'

the police did patrol.
And sometimes the customs man
was in along with the police,
and he would have pin-pointed the ones, you know -
well you could have been fined.'
                                'It all depended who you...'
'It depended - it depended actually who was on.
There was some of them could have been lenient with you,
but fair play to them,
there was little point in them being there
if they didn't have something to show for it.'
            ' It wasn't really large-scale smuggling, you know.'
'It was all personal stuff.'
                    'I didn't conceal it I'll be honest with you.
                    I went every Friday on the bus to Carrigans
                        and there was a wee butcher's shop
        and you could get down on one bus and up on the other
                            and it was always for meat -
                        because the meat was rationed.'
'And I had brought a roast one day,
and I was in the bus
and - I had it sitting on my knee, right enough -
and the customs man came up, and he looked...
well, you know the way a roast has a bone
and he did this...with the parcel...
and he felt the bone and I looked
and I made this wee innocent face of mine,
and I says, "It's...it's a roast".
And he looked at me a minute and he felt it again
and he tore the paper a bit and he saw the bone -
that's all I had, you know -
it wasn't really large-scale smuggling.'
                            'It was only for your own..
                            it was only for your own
                or for somebody that wasn't able to go down ...'
'And I said to him -
I think maybe because I was honest -
it was sitting on my knee -
and I said it was a roast,
an' he tore the paper, and, like,
you really shouldn't have been bringing even that over,
you weren't really allowed anything -
but I just sat looking at him
and he looked down and he says, "OK ", you know,
so, like, as I say, it all depended on...'
                            'It was going on all the time -
                            they knew about it, you know... '

Wetting the Tea

'Things were still tight.
Many a time we walked over the border
and many a time I walked back
with two pound of sugar down here
and a pound of butter in my pocket
and this and that.
And when you came home
the clothes were all blue dye off the blue bags,
the sugar bags
and the butter was run into oil -
it would have to be put into ice...'

        'Did ever you hear the story
        they told about the two women...'
'Actually it was the woman next door to us, Minnie...'
    'There were a couple of women
went down on a smuggling expedition to Bridge End,
    which was the nearest point there,
    and they got two pounds of sugar
    made up into two one pound bags
    and they got a half pound of tea,
    one of them got the half pound of tea.
And this one that got the half pound of tea
    was a very nervous type of person
    and she says,
"How am I going to get past the Customs man with that
    when he asks me have I anything to declare?
    I'll die of heart failure!"
    "Don't be daft," the other one says -
this was at the waiting room in Bridge End
    waiting for the bus coming.
    "Tell you what - come on in here.
    Now there's nobody about:
you put your half pound of tea up there
    and I'll do the same with my sugar".
And they did that, and they got into the bus.
    Just at that the customs man
comes on to the bus and he shouts, "Anything to declare?"
    And he was coming down
and the one that was nervous turns to the other and says,
    "Have you got the sugar handy?"
She says, "Why? What do you want to know for?"
    She says, "I have the tea wet..."

Toast

'We were talking the other night about...
you toasted the bread with the iron -
and intil the loveliest toast ever you got.'
                              'It made the loveliest toast.
                    you put the iron on top of the bread -
                         you came in with a bit of bread -
                      a sandwich of bread and butter -
                   and you put the iron on top of it,
                       and then we turned it over
                            and did the other side
            and you had the loveliest toast ever you tasted.'
'And the butter would have been
sizzling up round the iron, you know,
when the iron was sitting on the bread.'
                         'And the iron was cleaned after it -
                              you cleaned the iron.'
'And the loveliest toast ever you got.'
                              'We used to toast -
        I seen me with twenty sandwiches to toast for people.'
'They used to come,
the other girls that hadn't any...'
                         'And then when you went away
              some wee girl only in the door would have come
                   and, you see, we knew to test it first -
            and she would have just stuck it down on her piece
                         and it burnt the whole iron...'
'The iron then had to be all cleaned.'
                         'Instead a them cleaning it
                              they sneaked away
                        and never let on to you
            and then when you came in and lifted the iron
                         and started to work -
                              when you looked -
                   the whole collar was destroyed.
There wasn't even a thing to lower the heat or nothing -
                         you just plugged them in.'
'There was no steam - no steam in it .'
                              'No steam or nothing -
                         it stayed at the one heat,
                    it just got warmer an' warmer.'
'You had to just switch it on and off.'
                         'Or it would have got too warm...'

72

Half a'Derry

'Half a'Derry worked in the shirt factory.
I was fourteen on the Wednesday, the thirtieth of April
and I started work on the fifth of May
because they wouldn't start me in the middle of the week.
I had to start on a Monday.
But about three weeks before that my mother -
she worked in it,
my sister, sister-in-law and aunt all worked in Welch's -
and my mother would go to her boss and say,
"I have a wee girl that'll soon be ready for work -
in about three weeks' time".
And he said, "Well,
the week before she's due t'come in let me know".

And they just said, "Bring her in on Monday
an' bring a pair of scissors ".'
'That was for clipping the threads.
Everybody that went into the factory at first
went in as a clipper or a message girl,
and then after about two, three months doing that
then you started and you went to another job
until eventually you learned what was called a trade.
Now everybody said, "Always learn a trade"
because, at that time,
when the women had a trade
and then they got married and then they had a family,
well eventually they went back to work again
and they always had a trade to go into.'
'You'd always go into the same thing
or you could go into another factory with this trade.
I became a smoother -
that was a trade.'
'Well the trades in the factory were
side-seaming, front-stitching, pocketing, hemming,
button-holing.'
'Button-holing.'
'Fitting.'
'Fitting.'
'And then in the collar...
there was the inserting,
the patent turning, the collar stitching,
button-holing again -
well then you went from that to the examining
and then the next thing, next step was the laundry
that was a trade, the smoothing -
you had to smooth and fold -
and the boxing was a trade.'
'Well I was a smoother
but sure I finished up a boxer.
And one time somebody asked me
what I did in the factory -
in fact I was away on holiday and we were talking -
and it was somebody we met
one night when we were out
and they asked me what I did.
I said I was a boxer -
and they weren't too happy -
they thought I was being funny, so they did,
so they call them now packers -
and smoothers are now pressers -
but that's what they were when I learnt... '

74

The Fitter

'I worked in Hamilton's factory. I was a fitter -
I used to do everything -
I went in as a patent turner,
and my friend was working in Burns's factory
and she says to me,
"They're looking for fitters in Burns's". And she says,
"Why don't you go down and say you're a fitter?"
Says I, "Sure I, I don't know the fitting".
A fitter did the yokes, put the yokes on the shirt -
and what's this else - and the labels
and a patent turner is the cuffs -
turning them round for the cuff stitcher.'
                              'They have machines for that now,
                                  you see all that's done away with. '
'Everything's done now with machinery,
it was all hand done then.'
                                                 'I was the same.
                                I started up as a patent turner
                                and ended up as a turner out.'
'They turned her out.'
                                              'Turning out collars.
                              When they were stitched round
                      then we turned them out - like that there -
                          for the stitcher to stitch round them.'
'So I went down to the Burns's factory
and I says, "Ah hear you're lookin' for fitters?"
He says, "Aye are you a fitter?"
I says, "Aye, a' am."
And he says, "Well start on Monday."
And I went in and the forewoman came up
and she left me down a bundle of work -
she says, "There's some work for you,
when ye finish that," she says,
"just come up and get more."
And here was I, "Oh my God what am I goin' to do?"
An' the woman sitting beside me,
I says to her, "C'mere Missus, I don't know how to fit."
She says, "I thought you were a fitter?"
I says, "Naw, I'm just gonna chance me hand."
And she showed me how to do the fitting
and I just went ahead and did it.
She was from The Fountain, you see ...'

Billycans

'If you heard tell of a sale up in Woolworth's
you sneaked out and away up to it,
or if you ran out of cigarettes
you sneaked down the back stairs and out...'
                              'I worked in Glass's for a while,
                    and Mr Glass - he was one nice gentleman -
            he used to meet you on the stairs and he would say,
                          "Is there a sale somewhere the day?"
                                    And you'd say, "Aye."
                    "Well now, look, wait till I tell you -
                          don't be goin' out the morrow,
            because the big bosses are comin' from England
                    the morrow, and if they see you goin' out
                          you'll only get me into bother..."
            Well we wouldn't've moved the next day, knowing...
                    because he was that good of a man.
                    He would have let us out any time...'
'And there were no canteens.
And then us people from the country -
you see you couldn't afford to go to a café -
so we had all wee billy-cans,
and there was a gas ring down the stairs
and you queued up an boiled your wee can.
And there were no tea bags either.
You put a couple of spoonfuls of tea into it.'
                    'And there was a man came in one day to Welch's,
                          and he stood. He said he was in looking round.
                    And we were allowed, ten minutes before the time,
                              to go down, you see, to set on our tins.
                    And he questioned this woman about everything,
                          and here, in the Telegraph that night, it said
                    "*Music While You Work* was playing on the radio..."
                                    and it said, "All the girls
                          were running with their little tin cans
                    and their little pots and their little saucepans,
            and then they were singing." This all in the Telegraph.
                                    And the boss was raging.
                    He said he thought we had given an interview -
                          but it was the boy didn't let on who he was.
            He didn't let on that he was taking note of everything.
                    And he said, "There they were all sitting
                          with their little billycans..." '

76

Dead Horses

'I never really had a fight with anyone in the factory,
because I think, somehow, in those days,
everybody seemed to get on, you know.
Everyone was helping one another.
There were these, what they called "grabbers",
taking more work than anyone else.
You were paid just every dozen you did
I can't even remember how much it was
for a dozen of cuffing -
but there was a price for a dozen of work.
You got a ticket of the work, you see...
and you had to sew them on a book
and then leave it in the office.
And if you hadn't enough when you counted up
you would say, "Oh God, I haven't much this week..."
Then you'd have gone up and got more work
and taken the tickets off and sewed them in.
That was "dead horses".'
　　　　　'That's what they called them, dead horses,
　　　　　because the work wasn't done to the next week.
　　　　　　Then you went in on Monday morning
　　　　　　　　and you had to kill yourself
　　　　　　　trying to get the dead horses done
　　　　before you started earning for that Friday's wage.
　　　　　　　　It was just a vicious circle.
　　　　　All the time you were working trying to ...'
'There were no times like them, all the same.'
　　　　　　　'Not at all. And there was another thing...
　　　　　　　　do you see in The Fountain -
　　　　　they had bone-fires on the Twelfth of August.
Well, the people in the Long Tower used to come up
　　　　　　　　and join in the dancing and all.
　　　　　　　Now, I'll tell you something.
　　　　　　There were two boys came up -
　　　　　　one of them was a hairdresser -
　　　　　and they used to come up to our house.
　　　　Why they came up at the start was,
　　　　　when the Opera House was there
　　　　　　they used to have shows in it
and the people that came from England, you know,
　　　　　the different shows that came,
　　　my mother kept some of the show people,

just for the week and then they went away.
And you had a man that went to the station and met them
and brought them up to the house to you.
Well they used to come up after the girls, do you see.
They used to come up to our house every weekend
to see what kind of girls was coming.
And I remember, it was the Eighteenth of December
was coming up that week, and they were up.
And I wanted my hair -
no, the Twelfth of August it was -
and I was only about twelve, ten or twelve,
and I wanted my hair cut. And they cut it.
I wanted a Dolly Varden - it was the style -
a Dolly Varden they called it.
It was a bob haircut, and one of them said,
"Are you sure, now, that's what you want Lily?"
I said, "Aye...I want me hair cut like that..."
and he cut my hair. And the next day, the Twelfth -
that was the Eleventh Night -
they were up for the carry-on, the dancing and all.
And there used to be another girl came up - McLaughlin -
and she used to come up to our house too,
and she'd say, "Come now on up
to see if the dancing's started..."
The crowds used to come up and enjoy it.
And then on the Twelfth
they were out with their youngsters dressed up -
all dressed in their best clothes to see the bands
because I remember
this girl in the factory would say to me,
"What way's the bands going?"
because they used to go different ways,
and I'd say, "It's going Rosemount way this year..."
and she would say, "Oh that's grand -
then I'll go down to the Strand
and I'll see the bands all..." she says,
"I'll bring the wains all down to see it..."
'Sure the Royal Visits were the same - any Royal Visits.'
'Because the council always allocated so many tickets
to each factory and the girls used to sit waiting
to see who was going to refuse one.
They wouldn't refuse, nobody refused...'
'The names were put in a box and they were drawn out.'
'And the style -
there wasn't a shop in the town
had any style left.'
'They were round getting all the best.'

The Titanic

'Now, my mother was born in Bishop Street -
they had a pub just facing the jail -
that time it was Gilmore's,
then it ended one time
that it was The Crystal Bells they called it,
but I think my grandfather
was the first to open a pub there,
and he made coffins too -
he had a good business,
a big business -
his family were all in it,
because they were all carpenters.'

                     'You drank yerself to death
                         and he buried you...'

'I had an uncle, worked on the Titanic
when they were building it,
up in Belfast -
he did all the cabin work, you know,
all the inlaid and carving.'

                     'That's why it sank -
               because she was connected with it... '

'He married a Belfast girl, you see,
and they went up to Belfast to live,
and got the job in the shipyard.
That was when they lived in Bishop Street -
so my mother was an interloper
when she came into The Fountain to live.
When she got married she got a house
to live in The Fountain,
and then she opened a shop in it,
but when she moved
it was just Gilmore's,
her name.
It was one of these wee corner shops
and she sold everything,
groceries and all the different things,
but then she gave up,
because whenever the family started
they moved down to a hundred and nine.
I wasn't even born,
for that was away in nineteen hundred,
I'm the last in the family -

I'm the youngest in the family.
My father,
well, he was in the army
for most of his life,
but when he came out -
he was in the Boer War -
so you can guess how old they were...
my mother would be a hundred and fifteen
if she was living the day -
and then he was in the First World War,
and then when he came out of that
he was chauffeur to -
now, Tommy would mind him -
he was a lovely...
he was Sir Somethin',
he was one of the gentry in the town.
And then he got a job in Montgomery's,
driving a lorry

and from that
he went to the buses.
He never was off work - he never was -
never lifted one penny of dole money
in his life.
He worked all his life
till he was sixty-six
and he ended up in the NIC -
Northern Ireland Carriers.
Whenever the NIC was taken over by Ulsterbus,
they put him into it, driving a lorry,
and he worked there till he had to retire -
he should have retired the year before,
but he never let on
and they discovered then, you see,
and he was sixty-six,
so then...and he wouldn't stay idle,
so he went out and got a job in Lisahally,
as watchman down there,
and he worked there till he was eighty,
and he died when he was eighty
- eighty four when he died.. '
                    'He was one of the very lucky ones - he was...'
'We had a car whenever I was...that size.
Nobody else had a car.
It was an old Sunbeam,
and the hood went up and down
and whenever you'd have been out,
maybe, a lovely day,
we'd have been out for a run
he'd have taken us out on a Sunday -
and if it started to rain
he had to get out of the car
and put the hood up
and we were all soaked before he got it up.'
                         'I can remember them
                        taking me out in a pram -
                          a wicker pram -
            it was like an old-fashioned wheelchair,
                it was like a bath-chair thing -
                      it was a pram, but.
                    I can remember that.
          And my mother always painted it
          she used to change the colour of it
            she would have painted it white
                and then the next thing
        she would have painted it yellow...'

Poundies, Knobs, Chain Bones

'And do you see too, another thing, about the factories
I mind working in a factory
and the rats were running round -
big rats. I don't know where they came from,
but I remember one morning lifting a shirt out of my box
and the big rat just jumped up -
I'll never forget it - I ran squealing up the room -
jumped up on the bench, I don't know how -
I don't remember even jumping up on the bench.
But sure what could they do?
They knew, but they never bothered.
We used to stand on the toilet
down in The Parlour as we called it, The Parlour.'
                                    'You called the toilet The Parlour.'
'That was the toilets, was The Parlour,
and we used to be down having a wee smoke,
you see, you went down there to get a wee smoke,
and there was a kind of a ledge thing round it,
and we used to stand watching the rats round the ledge.'
                          'And you called the boss "The Man" -
you didn't call him "Mr Blair" or "Mr Boyd" or anything -
                you just said, "Oh, holy God, there The Man!"'
'In Hamilton's it was "Joe"and "Jim".'
                    'No, we called him "The Man" - called Mr Blair,
                when I started in the Star factory, "The Man" -
                    and if you were caught, you know,
                if he caught you coming in late or anything,
                                        "Where's The Man?"'
'We worked hard, now,
I mind, in Hamilton's factory, when I started in there,
on a Monday night you worked to nine o'clock,
Tuesday night you worked to seven o'clock,
Wednesday night you worked to nine o'clock,
on Thursday night you worked to seven,
and a Friday night you got off at six.
You had to go in on Saturday morning
and you worked to a half-past twelve on Saturday morning.'
                            'That was compulsory then
                and then I had to, when I got out of my work at six,
                    I had to get a bicycle and ride for an hour
                            on a bicycle before I got home.'
'That's why she's so slim the day.'

82

'We all had bicycles and we all came in on the bicycles
and then on the very severe mornings
we would have got a bus in.'
'And you used to come in on the wee train too.'
'And listen, we worked long hours them days.
You started at a half-eight in the morning
and you finished at half-twelve,
and you came home and got your dinner
and straight back to your work for two o'clock.'
'Two o'clock.'
'You got your dinner. You got a good dinner. Poundies...'
'All we got was a sandwich. '
'You see on account of me living here...'
'They were able to go home, but I wasn't .'
'Poundies. Potatoes pounded up.'
'Mashed potatoes.
You heat the milk and scallions in the saucepan
and then pour it over the mash potatoes
and a big lump of butter in the middle, and it runnin'...'
'Lovely! Oh dear! That's what we'd have got one day,
and maybe soup another day,
and chain bones out of the store -'
'Chain bones and cabbage.'
'Oh dear, they were beautiful, chain bones and cabbage -
pork meat and a bone, big bone...'
'And knobs.'
'You boiled the knobs with the cabbage.'
'And hawks...'
'Knobs - that was pig's knee - the pig's knee...'
'And the meat inside the skin was about -
about that thickness - but when you had it boiled
you took the skin off, and that meat in there...
and a wee bone, there was a wee bone.'
'Was beautiful...'
'And the meat was round the bone.
and there was only a wee bit of meat,
but that wee bit of meat was beautiful. '
'They always blamed that for the TB -
you mind the time it came out -
they said it was eating too much pork.'
'Too much pork - you see pork was cheap.'
'And you got a shilling's worth of parin's.
You went to Biggar's store for a shilling's worth of parin's
it lasted you all week - just bits of bacon.'
'Do you know a hawk, now? What they call a hawk,
they call it now a bacon joint,
well you'd have got one of them for one and six,

a hawk - and if you'd have seen the meat was on it -
and you took the fat off.'
                                'There's nothing on it now, Lily.'
'There's nothing, no. The pigs aren't as well fed, you see.
The pigs were fed with *brock*
that they used to come round the door
and collect from you.'
                                'When you were done with your dinner,
                                your mother scraped it all into a bucket.
                                And then the wee boys come round -
                                "Brock! Brock!" - round the doors.'
'And they took the bucket out and put it into a cart.'
                                'They had a wee cart with a bin in it
                                and they emptied your bucket.'
'That's what the pigs was fed with... '
                                'And whenever I saw a brockboy coming...'
'How did we eat it?
So whenever you're eating pork..'
                                'That was all kept for the pigs
                                when the brockboys came round.'
'How did we eat it?'
                                'And look at the potatoes - God bless us,
                                you never peeled a potato,
                because they peeled themselves when they were boiled,
                                you had to watch... '
'They were like big balls of flour.'
                                'They just parted company.'
'But, you see, I remember years ago
when I lived in the country,
this farmer refused to buy this stuff
that came in packets to set the potatoes -
fertiliser - and he said he didn't like anything chemical,
and his potatoes - everybody's potatoes were beautiful.'
                                'Organic.'
'And when he cleaned out the byres, you know,
that the cows were in,
when he cleaned that out he put it in a heap -
what they called the midden.
When they were setting potatoes the cart came
and they filled the cart out of that
and that was put on the drills
and that's what you're putting...'
                                'And that's why we had beautiful potatoes.'
'Sure they're going back to that way now -
they're going to start and go back .'
                                'Aye, organic - but they're very expensive now -
                                they were cheaper then...'

84

Khaki

'I didn't work.
I was only six when the war started,
so I didn't start working till nineteen-forty-seven,
but I remember my Mammy and my aunt talking
about "the karkies".
That's all they ever called them, "the karkies"...
apparently they were hard to sew...'
                              'They were a hard thing to work with -
        I remember them, all right, they were a kind of flannel.
                          I wasn't too keen on doing them
                       because whenever you were running
                   if you were put on the epaulettes, to do that
             you were put sometimes to do different jobs, y'know,
                            they were very, very thick there
                      and then the needle would break, you know,
            and then you would have to start getting in a new needle
                               you know that sort of way...'
'And then the Government Inspectors
would have come in to examine them.
I never ever saw this,
but I remember my mother saying
Government Inspectors would have come in
and examined work that was ready to go out,
to see that it was all right
but a lot of factories made "the karkies".'
                       'At them times you were afraid to speak.
                     You know nowadays the young people
                           would just turn around
                         and say to the bosses even,
                    but we were afraid to lift our head
                   but we always tried to do them well, like.'
'And I remember, when I went in,
well, it wasn't war time, right enough,
but you were doing shirts for the Air Force.
And the girls would have put in a wee note,
"If you're married never mind,
if you're single drop a line..."
that's true - and I would have maybe done it for a laugh
and put Kathleen's name and address on it
and I think somebody did it for one of the girls
and she got a great letter
from a grand airforce man in Singapore...'

85

The Donkey's Back

'I worked with my father, he was a carpenter.
We did repair work. We did roofs, fixed spoutings, anything.
We used to have a wee donkey,
and I used to be the donkeyman.
We used to cart the loads on the donkey,
but we used to always watch
that we didn't put it on too heavy for him.
We kept it in a gateway just across where we lived -'
    'There was an old stable in the Fountain, at that time -'
'It used to be Inglis's, at one time, the bread crowd,
and then, Sandy McGowan was the councillor then,
his brother, kept the coal,
they kept the coal in it, the horses and that,
and there was a wee stable for the donkey,
and coming up to the holiday times there was a friend of ours
used to let us keep the donkey out, away out past the Bolies,
and one day it went out, it was left out,
and we came back in
and somebody came over and knocked the door
and asked my father, "Is that your donkey across the street?"
"Not at all," my father said, "it couldn't be,
sure I'm only after leaving it out."
It walked the whole way in itself, right up...'
        'And up the steep street, up Wapping Lane...'
'All on its own. And when you went down the Strand
it was that used to going into Keys's
that you had to turn into Keys's, go up the yard and turn,
come out and then go on down the Strand.
It wouldn't pass going on down
without you going in and out.
It was that used to going in and out. Molly it was called.'
        'Molly, and the time the Americans came
                    during the war
      they all came up to get their photograph taken
            on the donkey's back, remember?'
'And the people used to come with their children.
It was supposed to be a great cure for the whooping cough -
three times under the stomach of the donkey.'
        'You didn't have to say anything.
        You just put the child three times -
somebody the other side caught it, lifted and lowered it,
and that was supposed to be a cure for the whooping cough.'

A Rickle

'I'll tell you one particular smell
that we always used to remember -
this was in Foyle Street - when they were clearing out -
there was McLaughlin, there was Buchanan
and there was Biggar's...'

                                              'Pork stores.'

'Pork stores - they used to do their own slaughtering
and of course they red out
when they killed the pigs and that, cleaned them out.
God save us,
the smell
would have knocked down bumbelly bees as they say,
and what always tickled me was,
there was a fellow there and we used to meet him -
you would have met him about three times a week,
and the cart full of guts and what have you,
and the smell was chronic -
and he would have been sitting up on the cart,
"Hello there, how are you doing?"
It never seemed to take a rickle out of him...'

                          'There was one fellow there,
                          I'll tell you what happened him.
                    He worked in Brown's Foundry, this fellow,
                          and he lost the finger and the thumb.
And they said, when they asked him what happened him -
                    he used to wear a glove stuffed with paper -
                    he worked a lathe in Brown's Foundry,
          and whatever happened he was working the lathe
                    and he was running the stuff up into it
and somebody came up behind and said something to him
          and he turned around and he lost the thumb...'
'Gurlo?'
                          'No, he had the twin thumbs...'
'Aw, that's right...'
                          'He had the twin thumbs.
And somebody else came along and saw the blood spurting
                    and said, "What happened you?"
                    And he said, "I done that there..."
                          and he lost the finger...'
'And there was another fellow they called Mibey Briars -
he had a great habit of saying "Mibey..."
so they called him "Mibey" and the name stuck to him..'

The Eliminator

'Although my father was educated,
my grandfather took him away from a job
with the County Council,
although my father, every year,
did part time work for the County Council office
for about six weeks
about the month of February or March,
he made up the rate books for them -
every year.
You got so much
for every hundred names,
and he did that at night in the house,
and you daren't blow your nose.
As a matter of fact,
when the electric came in
he still kept a gas thing for doing that.
He said the gas was softer on the eyes,
he always maintained that.
He had a table
and the gas was up above him.
We had electricity -
there was a name for it,
what's this you called it?
They had a name for it -
you paid so much a quarter
and you burnt so much
and if you put on too many lights
the lights went out -
an eliminator it was known as.
That was nineteen-thirty-two, you see,
and the Corporation owned the electric,
and they were trying to bring it in,
and they brought in this thing
that you were guaranteed light,
so many units,
and you paid twenty-five or thirty shillings a quarter,
which would have been big money at that time
and you were limited on the day.
Say you were limited to a hundred watts
for the whole house
and you put on a hundred and ten
the whole thing went out.'

Mickey wi' the Windmills

'Mick used to come round -
he went round all the streets -
but we waited for him to come round The Fountain.
He had a wee cart with him
and he had these windmills
and you gave him empty jam-jars
and he gave you a windmill.
And everybody, all the youngsters in the street,
were running as soon as they saw him coming
they were all into the house looking for jam-jars.'
            'Here Mickey...Mickey wi' the windmills...quick!'
'Aye, you know, "Have ya an empty jam jar, Ma?"
And then there was a whole fight
about who was going to get the empty jam-jar
to get one of these windmills, you see.'
                'It was just a thing made with a piece of wood
                    just a stick, you know, like a bundle of sticks,
                        and he had a wee nail on top of it
                            he had a thing on the top.
            And he'd - you know paper you paper the walls with -
                    well he had these things cut in four
                and he had a wee piece of cardboard like a cross
                and he'd a piece of wallpaper pasted on each one
                    and then we were all running about mad
                        round The Fountain with these sticks
                    trying to get the things to go round and round -
                            and our mammy looking...'
'They'd look at you now
if you handed them one of them things
they wouldn't know what to do with it...'
                            'We used to get hoops -
                        well it was always a wheel,
                an old bicycle wheel or something,
                            and a stick
                    and you played with that,
                        and then there was...'
'Tops - you know spinning tops.'
            'You put a piece of cord round, and a stick,
                    and you put it on your knee.
                    You had to buy those.'
'It was lovely too.'
            'It was great to get a spinning top...'

Dancing with The Bloods

'And then we had the pictures, you see,
we went to St Columb's Hall, the matinees in it,
and then The Rialto, we went to the matinees in it -
not the pictures that is now -
there was no sex then -
sexy pictures -
it was all just good clean pictures, *Casablanca*.
There was very little I missed, mind you,
and dancing films,
and *Gone with the Wind*, I never missed it.
It was on again on the television lately.
It brought me back.
They had a place on the Waterside,
The Tower, Bond's Street -
not Bond's Street - going over to the Waterside.
And they had a dance hall there, and we went to it -
but you had to be in at a certain time.
You ought to have seen us running over the bridge,
three or four of us -
you had to be in by ten o'clock.
I mind coming away down from Creggan
where we stole to The Bloods,
and you weren't allowed to go there,
you weren't allowed to go.
But it was always candlelights they had,
The Young Bloods they called them,
down the Lecky Road.
They weren't the same religion, you see,
in them times, and you would have been in trouble.
So we went, and we had a dance, just an ordinary dance.
We danced with them,
but when the time came,
on the coats and away home as hard as you could,
and we enjoyed it, but you daren't have said.
But we went then away up
to a hut somewhere in Rosemount,
but you had to be in at ten o'clock,
and I remember running down
and I was about five minutes late
and I stood saying my prayers at the door
before I went in,
but I still got thumped for being not in to time...'

90

The Penny Pictures

'And there was an old cinema
in The Fountain
in those days -
you know where John Bobs's was -
there was Granny Nutter
lived above John Bobs's -
The Cinema
was all I ever knew it as...
I never actually
saw films in it.'

'The Penny Pictures -'

'Now on a Saturday there,
you used to get a penny.
I used to go round to my aunt's
and beat her mats for her
and I got a penny there,

and my mother gave me a penny,
and we went down to Jimmy Doherty's bakery
in The Fountain
and we went in
for a pennyworth of broken pastry,
and he had a brown sheet,
and Jimmy
would have given you a fair load of that
and then you went down to the hall
and it was a penny into the hall,
the pictures,
and you were home and dry -
great altogether -
Saturday afternoon.
There was a man went round,
one of the boys
that went round,
that had a stick with him.
If you made too much noise
you got a clout.
They were silent pictures, you see.
And there was one man
you called One Belly -
he would have clouted you
very quick.'

      'And then there was another wee cinema
          down in Barrack Street,
            Daddy Byres's -
          he was a clergyman...'
'...aye, a Methodist, wasn't he?'
      'Well he had this wee cinema down there
      and he would have charged you a penny
            to get in
           and there,
      the usual spate, you know,
      you were getting excited -
        there was a cowboy
      coming up behind another,
    or a boy with a knife or something,
        and you shouted,
        "Look behind you!
        Look behind you!"
        That was too much -
    and the cinema was switched off
       and the lights went on
and you had to sing two or three wee hymns
    before he would put the film on again...'

Iris Stew

'My father was a great man for plants - she's laughing -
he loved plants
and it was only a yard we had
just a yard done with whitewash every year
and all cement
so he had the big sink, one of the big ones.'

                                                        'A jawbox.'

'A *jawbox*, full of clay
that was it -
but he had a big pot
one of the big porcelain pots
on the window-sill,
and there was one big flower in it -

well, it looked like a leek to me.'

'An iris.'

'Before the flower came on it
it looked like a leek.
So I was about fourteen the time.
Violet was married, and then I took over,
you see she married when I was twelve,
so I was starting work - I had started work -
and I was going to the dances and all.
And my mother said to me one Saturday morning,
"Ah, that dinner's ready, Kathleen," she says,
"will you - there are leeks out the back -" she says,
"will you cut the leek?" -
you'll never believe it -
"and cut it and put it into the gravy
and it'll be lovely". So -
I says, "That's alright, I'll do that".
And it came out near dinner time.
I thought, I better start.
I went out to the yard to look for these leeks,
but I couldn't see anything.
So I had seen the big...
says I, "Oh," says I,
"me father must be growin' his own".
So I says, "That's gran."
So I took - you'd never believe it -
I took...like when I think on it...'

'I can remember that like yesterday.'

'I took it out of the pot.
It was lovely and big and all too
and I washed it and I cut it up
and I put it into the gravy.
So my father - he was a breadman -
and he came along then.
I went up the stairs and I started to scrub the landing
you know that's what you did then
with the oilcloth, you see.
So I was scrubbing away at this.
Grand. And thinking it was great.
And I had gone down to get my father his dinner
when he came in.
My father says, "That dinner
was very nice, Kathleen," he says,
"is there any more?"
and I says, "Aye, there's plenty,"
and I gave him some more.
So I went back up the stairs again

and I started to scrub the landing.
And the first thing I heard was, "Hi, Kathleen,
did y'see was there anybody out in this yard the day?"
and I says, "Naw, naw...why? What's wrong?"
Oh dear!
"What's wrong?"
And he says, "My plant's away!"
And I says, "What plant's that?" says I,
and he says, "Me iris!"
And I says, "Is that...
was that it on the window-sill?"
And I says, "God!" I says.
And do you know this, the sweat run off...
"Oh dear," says I, "I put it in the dinner".
"What?
What?
WHAT?"
And if you'd heard him.'

     'Do you know what he said?
     Do you remember what he said?'

'I remember what he said,
because my father had a great habit of saying,
"Merciful you God!"
That was all he would say - "Merciful you God!" -
if he was annoyed with anything.
And all I heard my father saying was
"Aw, Merciful you God," he says,
"You're out there," he says,
"looking for boys
every night of your life," he says,
"and if you got one you would poison him!"
And he says,
"I'm goin' t'me work again -
Oh God..." he says,
"if I be sent to the hospital the day!
I'll be poisoned...I'll be poisoned!"
Well - me brother came in, Jim,
and Jim was great, you know
and he says, "What's wrong?
What's wrong?"
I was still up the stairs, you know -
I was afraid to come down the stairs.'

     'And I was behind the door.'

'And my father says, "Ah, that stupid...
up them stairs," he says,
"she took me plant...outta the...a lovely iris," he says,
"another month or two an' it would a'been flowered..."'

The Wake of the Goat

'Over the years William had goats,
Belgian goats.
Bessie I remember extremely well,
for as you were going past her you had to be very careful,
because you would have got a dunt on the backside
going past,
and he used to take them out the road
to God's Little Acre,
the spare ground out the Prehen Road, for a feed.
And Bessie died.
He had her for a long time and she died.
And one night we were coming down
and William called us to tell us.
The three of us run about,
and we were very pally with William.
He called us in to see Bessie -
he had Bessie laid out on the floor
and a candle at her head and one at her feet,
waking her.
Now they said afterwards
that he cut her up
and he put her down the sewer.
I couldn't swear to that,
but knowing the kind of him
I would say that it is possible.
You know that kind of a man...'

> 'There was no bonfires as we know them now
> in those days.
> It was a tar barrel set on fire -
> and everybody enjoyed themselves
> and it was great altogether.
> And then on a Saturday night -
> Madgie Campbell had a pub -
> it became Powers's afterwards -
> but then all the men gathered round there
> Saturday night,
> and there was always a wee bit of a spill.
> And there was a wee man had a wooden leg
> and they said that when the row started
> they used to roll him down the road.
> He would have rolled two or three doors
> down the road with the wooden leg.'

Paradiso

'Well you were made -
I wasn't made, for I was a teenager when I come to it -
in my 'twenties - wasn't even a teenager -
but it was your duty, you thought,
it was your duty that you never missed Church.'
                              'In our young days, certainly.
             I went to Sunday School and went into Church then
        and came out of Church, came home and got my dinner,
                      went down into the Salvation Army
                         to the wee meeting for children
                 came out of there and straight up to Church
                              for the Children's Service -
             that's five times on a Sunday you were getting -
                   nearly every youngster in The Fountain
                  whenever I was a youngster - all the same.
                                   And through the week
                 we would have gone down to the Baptist -
        they had a wee meeting for children down there -
        we went to the IOGT Hall for The Band of Hope
             and down to The Salvation Army another night
                 for The Sunbeams. We wore a wee uniform.
        And you joined the Brownies - it was a done thing.
        When you came to the age, you joined the Brownies,
        and then whenever you got too old for the Brownies
                              you went into the Guides.'
'If you didn't go to Church on a Sunday
and you tripped and fell on a Monday
you thought that's what happened you -
that's what you got for not going out on Sunday.'
             ' I knew a man was a great man in The Fountain
        he went to the Long Tower - what do you call him? -
        Danny Grant. And Danny used to go to eleven Mass
                    and he says that he used to have to go
                 half-an-hour before the Mass to get a seat -
                      he says that the Church was packed -
                              and he says now -
                         that was during the troubles -
                              "Now," he says,
             "I can walk in five t'eleven an' get a seat!"'
'Aye - he had the pub at our corner,
he was a Catholic and it was all ..'
        'The pubs all in The Fountain were Roman Catholic.'

97

'Kelly's was at the bottom of our street
at the bottom of The Fountain,
and at the top of Hawkin Street
Powers's and then The Paridisio
and then Danny Grant.'
                              'But Tom Power was a gentleman -
                                  Tom Power was a gentleman...'
'And so was Tommy Martin too.'
                          'And nobody interfered with them.'
'Tommy was wild good.
Tommy would have got up in the middle of the night -'
                          'Right enough. And if there was a death
                              Danny Grant was away to that house
                                  with a bottle of whiskey.'
'Anybody wanted an obligement
they went t' Tommy Martin.'
                                              'Oh aye.'

'Aye.'

Joseph Locke

'I knew Joseph Locke -
I knew him when it was Joseph McLaughlin,
before he was Joseph Locke -
he lived in Artillery Street,
and that was very convenient to The Fountain,
and that's where they lived,
the McLaughlins,
and Joseph was great for singing -
you know that song he sang,
'My heart is broking, but what care I...'
and he was always great -
I was very friendly with a woman out of Creggan,
a Mrs Young,
and he knew her well,
through her he knew me,
and we were always great friends -
always a great how-de-do for you
when he met you.
And he was a grand singer,
a great singer,
Joseph Locke.
Then, remember, he went to England
and he was a star over there with his singing.
He really had a magnificent voice -
his voice was like Caruso's,
a really good singing voice.
And he would have entertained everywhere,
all he had to do was stand up.
He was good fun,
Joseph Locke was good fun.
He was very popular in Londonderry,
very, very popular,
and he really was nice -
but the singing was the thing, you know,
if you got Joseph Locke to go anywhere,
the crowd went.'

Cold Turkey

'James Logue? They were the builders.
That Logue there, James Logue,
that was the grandfather.
That wee house that she lived in -
there was a gateway under her house
into his workshop.
It was all at the back.
Her yard looked down into his workshop.'
　　　　　　　　'The floor of our wee sitting room
was all humps and bumps with them carrying things in -
　　　　　　　　　　　　　　　　　　　ladders.
　　　　　　　　　　　　You would have been sitting
　　　　　　　　　　　　　　　and all of a sudden
　　　　　　　　　　the mat would have jumped up
　　　　　　　　with them carrying things into it.
　　　　　　　　But one year my sister won a turkey
　　　　　　　　　　　　　　and it was that big
　　　　　　　　　　　it wouldn't go into our oven.
　　　　　And there was a wee bakery down The Fountain,

Doherty's.
And Mrs Doherty said she would cook my turkey for me.
And I took the turkey down
and she said, "It'll be ready about six o'clock."
So she sent the delivery boy with the turkey,
but she said, "Next to Logue's."
Well, you see Logue's
lived round the corner from me in Albert Place,
and didn't they take the turkey
round to the house next door
to Logue's.
What did you call the two men?
The wee man lived by himself...'

'Not Lorimer?'

'Remember?
He lived by himself.
And the turkey was cooked and all
and the wee boy delivered the turkey.
So it wore on to six o'clock and seven.
There was no sign of my turkey.
This was Christmas Eve, remember,
and I went to look for the turkey,
and Mrs Doherty said, "Your turkey
was delivered
at three o'clock this afternoon."
And I said, "I never got it."
She said , "Aren't you next door to Logue's gateway?"
so they went for the wee boy,
the wee message boy,
and he was away to the pictures
with his pals, you see.
It was after six
and they didn't know
what picture house he was in,
so they had to wait
to the pictures got out.
In the meantime,
Mrs Logue came home
and went into her own house,
and she was only in
whenever the knock came to the door.
She didn't know anything about it, you see,
and the wee man said, "Mrs Logue,
there was a turkey left in here for you."
And when she saw it, cooked and all, she said,
"Dear, I cook my own turkey - that's not mine."
And he said, "Well, what am I going to do?"

And she said, "Wait till twelve o'clock,
and, if nobody comes for it, eat it."
And at five to twelve
Harry Philson was knocking on the door.
And there were four old men there together then.
And they were parlatic,
and they had the turkey
in the middle of the table
ready to eat -
in fact they said they ate the legs.
"Well," I said,
"It must have been a four-legged turkey,
for I got two legs."
And Harry Philson said -
I forget what age he said he was -
but he said,
"It's the first Christmas Eve
I never had a drink."
He spent from six o'clock
to five to twelve
looking for my turkey,
searching the county for the turkey.
And - the funny thing about it -
about ten or twelve years after it
I was at a party in the Memorial Hall
and Willie Lindsay was telling stories, you know,
things that happened,
and he said, "I remember
one Christmas Eve," he said,
"we spent
from six o'clock to five to twelve
looking for a turkey," he said.
"If it had have bloody-well run
before it was killed!
What was the sense of it running
if it was killed
and cooked?" he said.
And here was me,
I put up my hand.
He said, "Yes?"
Said I,
"Willie, that was my turkey."
"Might have knew!" he said.
And that wee man
was ready to eat the turkey -
but they were full drunk.
It was Christmas Eve.'

Hurricane Debbie

'Do you remember Hurricane Debbie?
'Member? One Saturday.
It was awful
and, aw Lord, we were standing -
the slates were flying everywhere,
and my mother kept saying to me,
"I wonder will your father be all right the day?"
And I happened to look out
and here was his plant -
and y'know these big heavy pots -
well my daddy had one of them.
He had a grand - a plant growing in it -
it was lovely too. Do you 'member?
A *sedum* it turned out to be.'

                                        'Oh aye, nice.'

'And it was lovely,
and I looked out, and I says,
"Ah, Lord, Mammy, me Daddy's pot'll be ruined".
Because the slates were flyin' everywhere.
So I went out and stood at the back door
till there was a kind of a lull.
Well I went out and pulled.
I couldn't even lift it.
I pulled it right over
and pulled it into one of the shades
and I stood in there till it went down
and then I ran back over.'

                                        'Aye.'

'My father come in from his work that night
and by this time it had died down, you see.
He walked straight in,
straight out the back -
"Ah don't suppose one of youse thought of me plants,
they'll be ruined!"
He never asked my mother and me
were we all right,
had we a slate on the roof
or anything.
I says,
"I nearly got kilt
wi' you an' your rotten plant the day -
it's over in that shade!"'

                                        103

Billiards

'A fellow called Harrison, opened a business,
he was a barber,
he's likely living yet,
Jack Harrison,
and he opened a barber's in a new building
at the corner of Hawkin Street and Lower Fountain,
and it was three garages on the Fountain side.
Welch's had a place underneath
and then you went upstairs
and there were two big rooms.
Harrison cut one bit off for the hairdressing,
well, for the barbering -
it was men's barbering then -
and then he had two snooker tables in behind that,
and he started off snooker.
Billiards would have been the thing then, of course.
They said it was more skilful -
the old people kept saying that billiards was the best -
but when you looked at the games

both were skilful, different skills.
It was more and more snooker in my time,
snooker was coming in in the forties.
The billiards lasted to nineteen-forty-six or so,
before the snooker was competitive.
Before that
you would have been playing in McAllister's time,
the famous James McAllister and Jim Denny
were the two top...
and then there was Alex Connors
and Victor Florentini. *
They were all billiard men.
Victor was a real character.
He owned a big shop down the Strand thonder.
He got up and he walked round the table,
studied it,
walked round and
studied it,
looked at it,
chalked his cue...studied it.'

'I'll tell you a bit of a laugh about it.
Victor came up to play, and Harrison took sick
and he had employed a chap called Paddy Nelis,
who lived down about the gas yard,
he was a barber.
And that showed you the thing then.
Pat was a Catholic, but nobody bothered,
he was a Catholic just,
Paddy Nelis,
right fellow.
And the boys came at him,
"Play!"
"Oh I canny play."
But they finally inveigled Paddy
into having a bit of a go,
and Victor came up to play,
and of course Victor went round the table
in his usual way.
So then a couple of days after it
Paddy was playing,
and Paddy
studied...
and walked round...
and round...
and studied it up and down...
mocking, do you see.
And whoever he was playing said,

*Fiorentini

"What are you doing, Paddy?"
"Augh sure I'm playing like the Ay-talian..."
'We used to go down on a Sunday -
Sunday was taboo,
everything stopped in The Fountain -
so then there was a billiard hall
at the foot of Orchard Street,
called McAlinden's,
it belonged to the famous bookie's,
it was friends of theirs were in Derry.
They had a bookies' in the bottom
and they had these two snooker tables at the top,
so that was the rendevous on a Sunday,
and occasionally St Columb's Hall,
they had four billiards tables,
but that wasn't just as popular with us
as the McAlinden's...'

The Medal

'Bob Wallace - he lived down in Albert Street
and he was a member of the Corinthians team -
he played also for Linfield, by the way.
There were two. There was another chap
owned a newspaper shop at the foot of Hawkin Street
on the corner, where McIntyre's have the shoe shop.
And there was another fellow, Tommy Jarvis,
and he also played for Linfield.
Wallace was a bricklayer for Colhoun,
down the Strand Road,
which was where the Strand Cinema was.
Colhoun's was knocked down to make the Strand Cinema.
It was built by a chap called James,
and he managed The Midland.
The Midland and The Strand was both the same company.
Well, Bob was working for Colhoun,
and Colhoun worked all over Ireland,
and apparently he was sent to down about Wexford,
as far as I know, and - this is just hearsay, now -
of course he was a footballer,
and you couldn't come home in them days,
and if you went down to Wexford
you stayed for a month or two,
and of course, being a footballer
he got mixed up with the locals
and he is reputed
to have won an All Ireland Junior Football medal.
He played with the local team
and then he got picked for the County, you see.
He was a big tough heavy man, he was about six foot odd
and he was made for Gaelic - no disrespect to the Gaelic -
and he won an All Ireland Junior, or Minor level.
It was common knowledge that he had done it -
he was just a hero, and as a hero he could have done it -
people in The Fountain at that time
weren't bitter or nothing -
there was just the odd one.
It must have been in the 'twenties
that he played for Linfield.
I don't think he ever left Derry -
he just must have gone up on the train on a Saturday.
I would say football wasn't as serious at the time -

maybe they didn't train so much.
And he lived in Albert Place for all my recollection,
and that's taking you back to the 'thirties.
And Tommy Jarvis - Tommy sold the newspapers -
I think he had played
for a crowd called the A Specials,
who were,
during the first Troubles,
they were brought in as auxiliary policemen -
what would we call them now? Reserves -
they were brought on then as full time men
the same as the Reserves now for the Troubles,
and Tommy played for them.
They were like the army, you know,
you could have been drafted to Enniskillen.
He lived at the corner of Hawkin Street -
the first house in Hawkin Street.
Well later on then they had another Corinthians
and they went down to play in Pat's Field
in the summer league.
Well that was down on the Foyle Road,
where the Star Factory was -
there was a bit of waste ground there
and they went down to play there.
I mind going down to see them,
and they played in it and won the league and all.
There was a fellow called Mickey McNutt.
He was one of the chief organisers down at Pat's Field.
Only thing was, there was a men's part.
The B Specials put a team in -
and there was a battle about them,
that's what ended the men's part.
They played a long time,
but whatever team they came up against,
the sectarianism came out.
But they had maybe had played
a couple of years in it type of thing.
I played a wee bit myself.
I played in the North West.
I played two cup finals in The Brandywell.
We played in the City Cup.
It was always played on Boxing Day.
I played the first time for Derry City Reserves
and we got beat five three,
the Navy at Maydown beat us five three,
and then I played for a team called Foyle Stars
and we beat Strabane two one in the final...'

Arches

'They used to make arches.
There were about three arches in The Fountain -
four. There were four.
You went round the bakeries and collected flour bags,
and then the women bleached them.
That was to make bunting. And then dyed them.
If it was a Twelfth of August you dyed them crimson.
But then we bought them one year.
They cost us over two hundred pounds.
And we used to go over to help when we were young.
We used to help them make the bows.
The bows were shavings, wood-shavings,
and they were cut out,
There was a man sitting with a big pot,
a big, big saucepan - and the dye in it.
And he had a chip basket.
He'd put the shavings in that
and then maybe call, "Who's next for a fish supper?"
And then whenever he put them out
we let them dry
and then we got them and turned them over,
you know, one end over like that,
and then you pulled this down and that made a bow.
And you put a nail through it, a wee nail,
so that then all they had to do
was hammer it on to the arch.'
                    'The men made the arches - the men in the street.
                              Wee Joe Ferguson was the boss.
            They called him "the boss" and he was only small.'
'Some of those arches were gorgeous.
They were that neatly done, you know.
They were perfect, just, the way they were done.
They put a lot of time into it.
The women helped. We made the bows.
We used to collect the money from people
to help to buy the stuff, the dye and the wood
to make them and the bunting and the flags.
And at the Queen's Coronation
they made things for up over each door, a shield.
And we collected the money
and they bought the material to make them,
the plywood and the flags on them.'

109

Bands

'They used to come up from Long Tower
whenever Lundy was burned.
I'll tell you something.
In the early days of the bands
they would have gone round collecting,
and they bought their musical instruments.
They thought nothing of...
there was a band,
a silver band,
Saint Columba's Band,
and they used to lend the instruments
to the No Surrenders,
and the No Surrenders
used to lend their instruments to them.
And the different bands all around
lent one another their instruments.
You see bands are bands.
The only time was
when somebody got drunk,
and they would have said,
"You're only an oul' Fenian..."
but that was in the drink.
But those two men maybe,
or two women,
went in and worked together,
did their shopping together.
It was only when, as they used to say,
whenever the blood was risen,
when it would come to the Twelfth
or something like that.
Now, in saying that,
when we talk about things being short,
and sweet coupons and things like that,
there was a shop in the Long Tower,
Owens's,
and you used to go down
with your sweet coupons.
And Peter Owens -
they used maybe to be able to get sweets
across the border -
they give you extra for your sweetie coupons.
And everybody - everybody -

helped one another.
Bishop Street was lined with shops
and you went into the different shops -
there was McGirr's
and there was Murray's - fruit shops...'
                              'Pubs and bookies, you know...'
'And really,
when I'm talking about fruit shops,
I mean good quality fruit shops.
And Mrs Murray had one son,
and he went in to the priesthood.
And she had the shop then
for long enough after.
And he used to come back.
Well, he knew everybody
out of The Fountain
and out of Bishop Street
and all the rest of it...'

The Bone Fires

'He was a big man
in Albert Street
and he would have got drunk
on a Saturday.
God, he wrecked the house.
His wife was the nicest woman,
and his family.
He had a nice family.
And everyone was afraid of him.
He was a big man like that film star.
What do you call that film star?
Quinn...is it Quinn?'

'Anthony Quinn?'

'No.'

'Broderick..?'

'No.'

'Anthony Quinn..?'

'No. He was an American...'

'Broderick Crawford?'

'No, no.
He used to act in cowboys and things
and you know, the ships,
like, merchant...'

'Errol Flynn?'

'No, no. He wasn't good looking -
he was a big brute...'

'Anthony Quinn?'

'Anthony Quinn - that's right,
Anthony Quinn.
And it was him that started the bone-fire
on the eleventh night of August.
And it wasn't the ordinary bone-fire.
You know the way the bone-fires now are
piled up with stuff?
He got tar-barrels -
so many tar-barrels -
and they were all put round.
And, my God,
the windows used to be all cracking.
Anyone that lived near it
their windows were all cracked
and the paint was peeling up,
and nobody ever said.
Nobody
would have come out and said,
"Look at my windows broke..."
That was all just passed over.
And after the Twelfth
their windows were put in
and they came out with a paint-brush
and painted their windows over again.
Because they were afraid of him.
They daren't have said anything to him.'

'I know.'

'But he was in charge of the bone-fire -
and then,
before the night was out,
he was full.
But he reared the nicest family...'

The Fifteenth

'Kathleen, my sister Kathleen,
lived in The Creggan
for nineteen years
and - ask Kathleen, she'll tell you -
she had the best neighbours.'

                  'She had the best neighbours.'

'And Kathleen never
would have come out of The Creggan
only the troubles.'

                  'Only the troubles started.'

'She'll tell you that yet.
And the street that she lived in,
the women
that she had living on either side of her
were the best neighbours.
One of the women's husbands
was the postman in The Fountain
for years.'

                  'Aye, Dennis, Bob Dennis.'

'Aye, and Kathleen
never would have left it
and I remember, we met them.
Now just last year one of them died.'

                          'Aye.'

'And David was over
with the car
and he took his father up to the house
and David and Bobbie,
that's Kathleen's two sons,
and her husband went up,
and Bertie says
he couldn't get over it.
When he went in
he says that one of the boys,
one of the sons,
because these boys
had been brought up with Kathleen's boys,
he says he just went over
and put his arms round Bobbie
and he was crying.
He hadn't seen him for...

It was really comical,
because one day Bobbie went missing
and Kathleen says to him,
"Where were you?
I've been lookin' for you this last hour."
He says, "I was up to the chapel
gettin' Holy Water for Grannie Ramsey..."- you know.
And Kathleen's youngsters didn't really know.'
                                    'They didn't, you know.'
'She brought them up home one night
on the Eleventh Night.
Now there was always something going on
the Eleventh Night
and of course
they saw all the flags,
and Bobbie says to Kathleen,
"Mammy,
is it the Fifteenth?"
To them it was just a great day
and that's the way they were brought up,
and that's the way the others were brought up then.
What it's like now, I don't know.'
                                    "Your religion
                                was your own thing.'

The Rabble

'There used to be a big man
sat in The Diamond.
I never knew what his name was,
but we never knew him as anything else
but 'Snuffytrunk'.
He used to sit
with a big snuffy trail
down his waistcoat
and he used to sit there
snuffing it up,
a half ounce every time.
But The Rabble was in The Diamond,
Spring and Autumn,
and it lasted to about five o'clock -
a two day fair -
and they sold everything in connection with farming -
ropes, anything at all -
and as well as that
there were all these itinerant people came,
fortune tellers
and Tie-the-boy.
Tie-the-boy
was one of these characters,
I don't know where he came from,
but they used to come in
from far and near,
these come-all-ye singers, as we called them,
singing their own songs -
that was the first time
ever I heard
The Gallant Forty-twa,
that's the first time I heard it.
It was an itinerant there
and he had made up the song himself
and he sang it himself.
This was the whole beauty of it.
They made up their song
and they sang it
to try to sell you the sheet,
and it was great.
And these boys -

oh, they could talk.
They would have sold you everything -
monkeys on sticks -
they had even the wee bird,
like a canary,
to tell you your fortune.
I think it was a penny or something
you gave them
and they opened the cage
and they had a wee stick,
and the canary hopped on up
and they brought it up
and they pulled out a drawer
and they had a wee fortune card
and the canary lifted a card
and that was your fortune -
whether it ever came to pass or not
I don't know.
I know that there was the hiring fair -
they were used mainly for that,
they came in and they hired them
for six months or a year,
whatever it might be.
And when it went on into the evening -
the horse fair was held in Butcher Street
and Magazine Street,
this is at The Diamond there,
that's where the horses were bought and sold,
and always -
there were plenty of pubs about there -
then there was the fight at night,
you know,
the coats trailed,
as they called it,
then there would be the odd battle there.
And that went on every year
without fail.'

A Fallen Palate

'What about the fallen palate?'
'Aye, if your palate fell,
she got pepper on a spoon
and she got a hold of your head and she pulled your hair,
and you says, "Aaaaagh"
and she threw it in your throat.
I'm telling you, your palate -'
'It worked all right, but it was pretty painful.'
'Them was all cures.
But my mother would never have been cruel or anything,
still you got a right tip if you did anything,
but she was doing that just for the good,
for to help you, for the palate of your throat.
There was a lady up the street did it often.
It was common then -
you know the way, now, long ago
there were things and you wouldn't hear tell of them now...'
'And, do you see, it's different now with the bins.
You see then, whenever the ash bin men came round
they only came only so often -
it was what you called an ash-pit you had,
and the ashes were all just thrown in it
and the men had to come in
and dig it into bags and take it out.'
'Well, my mother had papers
right from the thing to the very front door to let...'
'There was no back door - we were up against the Wall -
the Derry Wall was part of our back yard actually
and the house we lived in, one hundred and seven,
there was an opening went away in under the Church and all,
but we didn't know about it.
It was built up with brick.'
'It was supposed to be, at the time - my brother found out -
he lived in a house further down,
he lived in a house, seventy-one,
and there was a secret passage to the Cathedral Church
from the time of the Siege.
And how The Fountain got its name -
there was some kind of a water thing in The Fountain,
and they used to come right out to get the water then,
and that was how The Fountain got its name,
and it never changed.'

Seventy-seven

'I was in the shop having a cup of tea
and the lady said to me about the times
and the troubles and all,
"But," she said, "Isn't it lovely now that we have a house
that we have an inside toilet and bathroom".
And she was asking me where I came from
and I said, "The Fountain".
Naturally enough she knew my religious persuasion,
and she said, "You know it was so different from you".
I said, "Excuse me, madam,
we had to go outside to our toilet,
and the only bathroom we had
was one that my husband had to build by himself".
She was amazed by the things that I was telling her,
because her concept of us was that we had money
and that we lived well, and we didn't -
we lived just from week to week.
She assumed that because we painted and papered...
and my husband
practically built our house in The Fountain.
They had no idea.
Probably there were people making money,
but we didn't know about it,
because we didn't mix with them.
We were just the ordinary working class people
who just cared about each other.
But the friendship in The Fountain
was something that I don't think will ever -
you'll never get anywhere else -
the caring for each other.
We just cared about each other.
In fact the lady across the way,
whenever I was having my children,
always came over.
My children were all born in the house,
my six children were born in my house in The Fountain,
and my sister's three children - she lived in Emerson Street -
she came over,
and her three children.
I was midwife to everybody.
There were nine children born
in the big front room in The Fountain,

and now I couldn't even buy Dettol at the moment
that I don't think that somebody's going to go into labour,
because everybody seemed to be steeped in Dettol -
it was Dettol, Dettol, Dettol...
But I loved every brick in The Fountain - every red brick -
my name was even carved out
on one of the bricks in The Fountain -
KK, because it was Kathleen -
my name was Mary Katherine,
but everybody called me Kathleen.
But I loved it and I cried that night
that we were leaving number seventy-seven -
and the night that we were to leave
they hadn't all the furniture out
and I said to my husband, "Take you the children up,"
and I stayed in the house that night all by myself.
But somebody else came into my house -
I think it was Olive Little -
they were moving the people
from all the different side streets -
when you think of the wee crotchety houses
in Fountain Place,
how people raised a family in them
I shall never know... '

The Water Cart

'In those days there were no bins as you know them now -
it was the dumpit, as we called it
out at the back of the house, next to the toilet,
where all the ashes were dumped in.
Then once a week the dustmen came,
and they were the old-fashioned style,
they had the trousers tied here at the knees
with a bit of cord, which, I found out afterwards,
was in case there were any rats flying about.
And they had ordinary zinc baths
and there were two men in
and they filled the baths
and the other two carried them out
to the horse and cart outside -
just an ordinary side-car, an ordinary cart,
a horse and cart, a trailer,
and when it was full there was another one -
it went away to the dump wherever it was
and the next one was the same thing.
We took our rubbish out in a zinc bucket -
if you were redding out the ashes or anything like that,
this wall was built about three foot high
and you dumped it into that
and every week they cleared that out,
shovelled that out and into the cart and away with it.'
                    'And there was an old horse-drawn water cart
                              came round in the summer,
             and it was our delight to get the shoes and socks off
                                   and out after that.
                         It was like a tank built on a cart,
                              a water tank, you know,
                         and there was a pipe came out
                         and it was perforated with holes,
                                   water holes,
                         and they turned on the water
                              and it sprayed out of this
                         to damp the dust in the street -
             there was no tarmac or anything in those days -
                    cobbles and just ordinary rough -
             it was just like a country lane would be nowadays -
                              there were no cars,
                    a car would have been something of a marvel.'

The Mangle

'In the Fountain
we had good houses -
they were four bedroom houses,
and where I lived,
we lived up at the top of The Fountain
about three doors up
and Tillie and Henderson's girls
used to come up and down
to their work every day -
well they waved to us,
and we waved to them.

There was no such thing
as trouble and rioting
and things like that.
We had a very good mother
and father.

In them days,
if my mother made a big pot of soup
and she knew families
that just maybe
couldn't afford it,
my mother sent soup to them -
many's a time I carried soup
to different people's...
nothing was ever wasted -
it would be thrown out now
but not on them days.

Our house in The Fountain,
we had a back yard,
and they had a shed
at the bottom of it
that my father had built,
where the big mangle was kept.
A big, big mangle
with a handle going round on it.
In fact
I got my hands caught in it one time,
and my father -
there were cousins of mine
up staying,
playing with the boys at the back -
and somehow
I got my hand in the mangle.

Well, my father
stood at the back door.
They all run.
I squealed murder and they run,
and my father thumped them all,
and my mother says,
"Why didn't you
go out
and let her hand
out of the mangle?"

But he says,
"I got the culprit," he says.
"Nobody done it,
but I got the culprit,
for I thumped them all!"'

The Range

'Wednesday, I hated it.
I remember going home on a Wednesday for your dinner -
you didn't have school dinners,
and you didn't have a lunch,
you had your dinner at twelve o'clock -
I used to hate going into the house.
That was range-cleaning day
and everything was covered in black lead
and the thing was out and it was cold,
especially in the winter
because the fire couldn't be lit until the range was cleaned,
and the house, to me, was as bare,
the bit of fire gave a bit of warmth to it...

But my granny lost three sons,
as she thought, at The Somme.
My granny had a family of ten plus two -
one died at childbirth
and the other died as a young infant -
lost three sons at The Somme.
But the story is
that she was going up to McGowan's shop
for a pint of milk -
I still get vexed when I think of this -
this was about two or three weeks after The Somme,
and she was coming down with a pint of milk,
and somebody shouted, "Mary! Mary!
You're wanted at the foot of The Fountain!"
And she couldn't see.
She could see sort of a crowd.
Jimmy, one of the sons - missing believed dead -
was standing at the foot of The Fountain
and the army uniform was half hanging off him
and the boots were half hanging off him
and he had no memory of how he got up though England
back to The Fountain.
And he died when he was quite young.
But her son Jimmy
was at the foot of The Fountain,
and my son is called James.
She was very strong, my granny.
She was very strong.'

The Fall of Babylon

'We used to have a galvanised square tank
out sitting in the yard,
and it wasn't covered or anything,
and there was a big galvanised bath
you were washed in,
and there was a tap in the sink.'
                              'We had "jaw-boxes",
                    what they called "jaw-boxes".'
'Big square crockery sinks -'
                              'And in those times
                there were never any strange diseases.'
'The only thing I was thinking about
was the old lady,
the woman they called
'The Fall of Babylon'.
She used to preach round the streets,
and she lived next door to us,
and one of our family -
this was away before we were born -
died with scarlet fever.
And the house had to be fumigated.
And she went round
telling everybody
that my father tried to poison her,
because the walls were porous,
and this went through into her...
and she swore till the day she died
that my father had tried to poison her.'
                              'And, do you know this,
                              the boy that died,
                they nearly broke their heart about him,
                              and he died
                        because they didn't know
                              what diphtheria
                              actually was then.'
'They took you out to the Foyle Hill Hospital.'
                              'It was a killer then.'
'Once you went in there
that was the end of you -
they did their best for you,
but they only knew so much in those days -
nowadays it's different.'

126

After Babylon

'There were people came after that,
by the name of Kirk
came to live there.
At the start off
I could nearly name everybody
that lived in The Fountain
in those days.
There was Taylors
in a hundred and eleven
and they had a brother called Tommy Tack,
as we knew him,
slightly deformed,
but Tommy had a wee horse and cart -
pony and cart -
and he sold vegetables
and that's what he made his living at.
Quiet family, very quiet.
And then
after Babylon went out of that,

Lily Barrett,
as she was then,
their family was reared in it,
the father Bob and the mother Lizzie,
they were reared in it.
They lived in a hundred and seven,
then Kirks
was a hundred and five,
the Youngs
was a hundred and three,
McCallions, Jack McCallion,
man they called Jack McCallion,
worked in the power station,
he lived in a hundred and one.
And there were Browns,
the baker people
and there was Evans's or Boyds,
and then there was Lizzie Hunter,
and the Walkers
lived in the next door to that.
Then they went to live in St Columb's Court,
next door to the Cathedral,
they went to live in them houses.
And then there was Crawfords -
there was another family
lived next to Walkers,
and then there was Orrs
and then Crawfords.
Then there was Ben Rutledge.
Ben Rutledge had a carpenter's shop there
and Ben Rutledge -
there was a football team
in the Fountain area,
The Corinthians -
and Ben was a great supporter of The Corinthians.
And he used to smoke cigars -
and if there was a goal scored against them
Ben nearly swallowed the cigar -
he nearly would have cut his own throat.
You went on down then
to Francis Stewart's wee shop -
Willie Stewart -
and then there was Jim Gallagher,
who was the -
when the old baths was in Rossville Street,
and that's going back a few years,
and Jim Gallagher was the attendant there.'

The Walls

'When my mammy and daddy got married
they lived in rooms.
Everybody did that.
People let off rooms
to everybody in those days
they all moved into rooms, you know.'

                'Mrs Kelly across the street
              let my mother and father live with her.'

'My granny only had a very small house,
and that house across the street
had two bedrooms
and they had an attic, you see,
which was great,
so my mother had a room off Mrs Kelly.
They all did that, you see,
that's the way everybody started -
you had a room
and you would cook maybe,
share her kitchen.'

                    'And sit up in your own room.'
'And then, number fourteen
it was going empty -
the old shoemaker
he must have died,
I think.'

                            'Aye.'

'He died.
There was an old shoemaker lived in it,
and my mammy says
- he did shoemaking in the house -
and she says he had a donkey.
He used to take the donkey
out the back yard -
right through the hall
out the back yard.
Anyhow my mammy says
Granny came over to her one day
and she says,
"Florrie,
that house is goin' t'be empty",
and my granny
went down to the rent office
and told the man about it,
and she says it was in a terrible state
and my mother always told me
they got the house for cleaning it
because he made his...'

                      'Shoemaking. '

'He did his shoemaking
in the front room
and my mammy says
he had a big bath of water
and there was all his tools -
you know what a shoemaker's shop's like -
and then he just he didn't use the upstairs at all,
he just slept in the other room
and he worked you know -
just a man on his own.'

                    'That explains it.'

'Well, doesn't it?
So they said that
if they could get it cleaned out
they could have it.
So, I remember, my mother told me
that they started,
and when she saw the house she says,

"Oh, dear God, I'm lost..."
He says, "Florrie, go you over to your mother's
an' stay in your mother's an' I'll..."
and he worked away,
and she says he took
seven bags
of dirt out of that house
before they could even start - you know,
old bits of leather and
just old stuff that the man had,
and they - it was distempered
the houses were distempered -
and it was Royal Blue
and that's true.'

'That's true.'

'Anyway, they cleaned it,
got it all cleaned out,
and got whatever bits and pieces they had
and got into it,
and that's how they got that house.
Well then,
as the years went on
and they were papering it
and what not,
my brother-in-law was papering it,
papering the hall
for my mother one year,
and he decided to strip the walls.
And I was sitting on the stairs
watching him.
And he was pulling all this paper off,
and he stood looking
and he says to me,
"Come 'ere t'you see this,"
he says,
"You think that's the wall?
Well it's not," he says,
"the wall's
two an' a half inches behin' that,
there's that much paper on it."
So that's how my mother got the house.
If you saw one going empty then
you just went to the rent office -
it was Magees owned all those houses
and you just went down
to the rent office
and put in your spoke, you know.'

The Streets

'We lived in number fourteen,
and my granny lived in eighteen
and my aunt lived in nineteen - Albert Place. '
'She was in Albert Place. I actually lived in The Fountain.
I was born in The Fountain. My grandfather
was born in The Fountain, although...
whenever his father went down to register the birth -
they had lived in what was called The Cage
in Linenhall Street, down beside the YMCA
and they had moved into The Fountain -
and whenever my grandfather was born
his father was drunk when he went to register him -
he registered him as living in The Cage in Linenhall Street.
And May's granny and my grandfather, they always met up
together and you would have heard the two of them, saying
"Ah, James, we were the on'y two that were born
in The Fountain. The Fountain canny claim
any of the rest o'them". In those days, you had to be
born in The Fountain to be Fountain. '

'You see The Fountain was a big long street
and there was one, two, three, four, five, six streets off it.
There was Albert Street, Albert Place, Fountain Place,
Victoria Street, Wapping Lane and Clarence Place. '
'And Hendron's Close and the Lower Fountain
and then there were the different streets off Wapping Lane -
there was Kennedy Street, Henry Street, George's Street. '
'Aubery Street .'
'Aubery Street and what do you call the Row,
where wee Maggie lived?'
'Major's Row. '
'Major's Row - it was fairly dense, you know.
Whenever I talk, whenever I'm talking about The Fountain,
I mean The Fountain from Bishop Street straight through
to Carlisle Road, although, taking The Fountain as
from Bishop Street to Hawkin Street now -
my end of The Fountain went from Bishop Street
up to Fountain Place. The other area was
from Fountain Street - Fountain Place,
taking from the top of Victoria Street
to the top of Wapping Lane, and then there was the area
from Wapping Lane to Hawkin Street
and then there was the Lower Fountain
from Hawkin Street down to Carlisle Road, it was.
Each group of houses had their own identity -
they had their own people that they went to.
Albert Place, they had their own people
that they identified with.
But we all went to school the same.
Now May went to First Derry -
went t'First Derry Church -
then there was the Cathedral.
There were people, then, Saint Augustine's,
there were people, then, Carlisle Road -
we all went to our own church schools
and we all went to our own churches, now.
I wouldn't actually have thought,
unless it was something special,
"Now I'm goin' to First Derry on a Sunday" -
nor she wouldn't have thought on going to The Cathedral,
unless for some specific reason,
although we were all close, as I say.
When I talk about May's granny, Emma -
Emma used to come up and knock at the door
and she'd shout, "James, are y'in?"
and the two of them would have sat about
and sat and talked about when they were young...'

The Half Moons

'Always.
And this half-moon at the front step.
Every morning
I did the brasses,
did the half-moon,
washed the window-sill.
You went up and maybe
did the upstairs as well,
and this was done
every day in life.
Washed your hall, polished it -
we had the lino.
I was just saying
to one of my kids the other day.
I've got a scrubbing brush
that I bought
when we came out here,
and a sweeping brush.

My sweeping brush
is only just finished
and the scrubbing brush
is still OK -
and in The Fountain
I would probably
have gone through a scrubbing brush
every month.
We scrubbed and...
that's just what we did.
And everything was done
on a Saturday night.
The shoes were brushed,
their clothes were all left out,
you cooked the dinner -
it just had to be heated up -
and there was nothing actually -
you wouldn't even have knit
or sewed
on a Sunday
when my kids were young.
And they go shopping now -
it seems so odd.
We just didn't do it.
Everything
was done on a Saturday night.
The thought of washing
or hanging out a washing
on a Sunday was just
- oh dear -
just wasn't done.
Or lifting an iron
to iron anything.
Sunday was a day of rest
and Church
and that was it.
You got spiritual help...'

The Dark Lane

'That was the real name, the Dark Lane -
that was down off... '
                                        'Barrack Street.'
'Down Barrack Street you went to it... '
                                        'They're all away now.'
'It took you down into Stanley's Walk. '
                                                'Aye.'
'Well they used to say there were ghosts, like, and all.'
                                        'We never saw any.'
'There used to be a cinema, you see,
a big hall in behind them houses,
and it ran away up... '
                                                'Aye.'

'And they used to say it was haunted.
We used to go to the pictures there
whenever I was wee.
We used to go down to the pictures in it -
silent pictures, you know -
I don't think they had a piano -
it wasn't swanky enough.'
                        'Nobody played the piano,
                unless they wanted money and that.'
'It wasn't swanky enough for a piano.'
                                'But they just said -
                        there were an odd one heard...'
'Aye, well the house, do you see,
the house next door till it, Bennett - Beattie's...'
                                                'Aye.'

'Well, Mrs Beattie always said
that there was a ghost in her house -
she always swore -
because she said there was a certain time every year
there was always blood on her wall.
One of her rooms - they saw blood -
and they would have washed it off
and the next year it would have...'
                                'Been back again.'

'Been back again -
I mind my mother telling us that...'

The Holy Picture

'Oh, it was the redevelopment.
The troubles would never have moved us.
We were as great then with the people as ever we were,
for we used to work together.
There was one girl from Creggan
always used to say to me...
we used to dress her up in the factory,
and we put a sash and all on her.
It was Hunterites* that was in the factory,
and we marched her in singing *The Sash*
and she'd always say to me,
"You'll get me excommunicated!"
she says, "I'll be excommunicated!"
But she was a good friend, she was just a highlight
of the factory, because she was really good fun
and she enjoyed a joke and all.
I said to her one time -
her husband was bad with his chest, with asthma -
I said, "What does you husband do about his asthma?"
"Oh," she says, "He sleeps in the other room!"
"Well," I says,"What about the union of man and wife?"
"Oh," she says, "I fell out of that union years ago!"
Till she actually died we were great friends.
And one day my brother came to me -
he was working down at the East Wall -
and he came to me and he said,
"We were redding out the day," he says,
"and there was this lovely picture," he says -
it had a great frame on it, oh, the frame was marvellous:
it was a picture of the Sacred Heart.
He says, "I didn't like to destroy it,
maybe you'd know somebody to give it to?"
So I said, "Right. Bring it to me!" And I went in to work
and I got all the wee girls and I said,
"Come here quick - go and get me paper,
brown paper, till we wrap up this picture".
Wrapped up the picture, put it on my friend's desk
and in she came and she says, "What's that?"
Says I, "It's a present for you."
She says, "What is it?" Says I, "It's a picture."
"Aye," she says, "What of?" Says I, "Well," -
she was going to America for a holiday -

*Hunter Wrights

"You're going to America, and I always said
I would give you a picture of William
crossing the Boyne," says I.
"There he *is*, *there* he is!" says I.
She told me afterwards, she says,
"I just said to myself, I'll not break it,
but I'll just throw it overboard".
And then she opened it and she said,
"My son's got a new house
and he couldn't have got a better present than that."
And she was telling me afterwards then,
the wee boy was out with the children in the street
and he started to curse,
and they got on to him, and his father said to him,
"You musn't curse in front of the holy picture".
And the wee boy says,
"Well, I'll go out to the scullery and I'll curse out there".
She was good steam, so she was...'

Breakneck

'My daughter came home from England
and she had the wee boy with her,
and he was only about three.
And we were down around Foyle Street one day
at the market.
And there was an ice-cream van, you see.
And I wasn't thinking, and I said,
"Gene, d'you want a poke, son?" He said, "No...no..."
and I said, "What's wrong with him? Is it the car?
What's wrong with him he doesn't want a poke?"
And my daughter said, "She means 'cone'...ice cream..."
And he said, "Oh yes, Nan, yes. I thought you meant 'poke'!"
And we came off the bus in John Street one night last week,
and I said to May, "Will we go up Breakneck Steps?"
And she said, "Aye, might as well."
So we went up Breakneck Steps.
Do you know where the bus stops at John Street -
the first bus stop?
It's at the foot of those steps. And you walk up those steps
and it leads you up to Carlisle Road.
Well that was always known as Breakneck Steps.
It's all fixed up now, isn't it,
nice, with a handrail and nice even step?
Before it was all rough.'
       'You would have broken your neck on it.'
'And I happened to say that to one of my grand-daughters,
and she said, "Where's that?" And I started to explain to her,
and she said, "I never knew there was such a place."'
       'We saw the name up that night, what was it?'
'Carlisle Pass.'
       'Carlisle Pass.'
'And I said to Kathleen, "I'm nearly sixty,
and that's the first time I've heard the right name for this.
Carlisle Pass."
It would take you from Carlisle Road
right down into John Street, you see.'
       'All we ever called it was "Breakneck",
       and nobody ever called it Breakneck Steps.
They used to just say "Breakneck" - "Aw, we went down
       Breakneck..."
and everybody would know what you were talking about,
       you know.'

Grey

'Everything was grey.
Everything in the winter was grey.
The houses were red brick,
but very often there was a low cloud,
you know Derry weather - dull.
My granny, being a widow woman at that time,
always, at all times, wore the black dress
with the cross-over apron,
and her idea of getting dressed up -
after the dishes were washed at night,
she came in, washed her hands and face
and the outfit wasn't changed,
the black dress stayed on, the clean pinny,
the clean cross-over pinny, was put on.
And this was very much the older woman.
Now, the time I was a child,
you have to remember my granny reared me
when she was a woman of seventy-three.
Seventy-four.

She took a new baby at seventy-three, seventy-four.
My aunt May didn't dress very brightly,
this school was not as you see it now,
as I remember, it was that dark green -
you know that public building green type of walls.
But we were allowed out to play on the outer playground
there below the Cathedral,
that was on a good day,
but on the dark days or the wet days,
that inner, downstairs, closed-in playground,
that's where we played -
a whole tribe of youngsters galloping round,
boys and girls together, all thrown in together.
By the time it got to the fifties
the boys and girls were all lumped in together.
This idea of everything being grey...
our house was always spotlessly clean,
but again, the decor - this was the way it was -
I can remember, up until I was, I think, eight or nine,
the black range -
the decor, Victorian style, was dark.
Maybe it was because it wasn't as easy to keep things clean.
But the summer - now, the summer lightened things up.
But another memory I have
is sitting over at one of the sides of The Fountain.
I was only a wee girl with sandals and a dress,
and I remember looking up at the sky -
you couldn't see much sky
because the houses were fairly close together -
and it was the most beautiful day -
I can remember it was a lovely day,
but I still had to sit...you couldn't get into the sun -
whether this is symbolic or actual -
you couldn't get into the sun
because the shadows of the house
overcast any bit of sun you had.
Do you know where we used to go to sunbathe?
Do you know the graveyard?
That was the nearest bit of grass.
That was the nearest you could get to a bit of grass.
Our back yard - my granny had a wee tree growing in a pot
and it was, I remember, nasturtiums,
planted in a window-box or a wee box along the wall
or even literally where the concrete met the wall,
there were a few wee nasturtiums growing up,
so the nearest grass, openness, the sky, sun,
the playground - our playground was the graveyard...'

Bog Bean and Sulphur

'We had a good, happy life in The Fountain,
and when the boys got up they put in a bathroom -
it was a gas geyser then, and we had the bath in -
but in our early days
we were all washed in a tin bath on a Saturday night
a big bath in front of the fire:
I was put in first, I was the only girl then,
and then the boys:
and we never had any diseases -
we never had any diseases at all, you know.'
                    'When it came to the Spring of the year,
            my father he used to get this stuff called Bog Bean
                                             and sulphur,
                  and he made up a concoction of this -
            talk about - and it would have poisoned you,
                                    and you had to drink it.'
'It cleansed your blood...'
 'It was supposed to work through your blood - Bog Bean.'
'Bog bean - from the Free State it was brought -
and he did it with boiling water...'
                    'He boiled it, you know - it was a plant.'
'Aye, there was supposed to be a cure in it.'
                                            'There was.'
'And he boiled it and we were made drink it
to clean our blood.'
                'Sulphur and treacle was another cure.'
'We got that to kill the worms...no -
what did we get to kill the worms? -
we got that to clean our blood.
At certain times of the year
we got everything that was going.
My mother had all these doses in -
we were all healthy.'
                            'Best dose of the lot
                no matter if you had a sore finger,
            your mother gave you a dose of castor oil -
                    that would have cured you...'
'You wouldn't have spoke,
because if you spoke at all she was away for the bottle
and you just got dosed with it, so you just shut your mouth.'
                                        'This is it -
                you had to be bad before you complained.'

The Barber's

'Oh aye, the barber, he's dead too.
Aye, they all went in there.
I mind taking my wee boy down to get his hair cut
and I sat for the crack, for it was that good.
They were talking about old times
and talking about this thing and that.'
                'Somebody would have started about something
 and one word led to another - more like going into a pub.'
'More older people, you know,
middle-aged men and old men
and they would used to be sitting talking about old times
and George was cutting all their hair - ninepence a time.'
                'And there was sometimes they would have said,
    "Aye, do him there next, 'am time enough!" you know -
                                nobody was in a hurry to get out.'
'Because they were enjoying the crack.'
                'Wasn't that the place the man cut his throat?'
'Aye.'
                                'That used to live there?'
'Of a Christmas morning?'
                                'Aye - cut his throat.'
'And the thing was, his friend -
I was invited down to Maudie Woods's for my tea - or was it?
Was it my tea or my dinner, that Christmas?
And we were in...
a friend of his again - do you mind the wee man?
The wall - lived up the wall there, up beside
the First Derry School - he was a friend of his, you see,
and the police came to the door
and we were sitting at our dinner
and the policeman said - looking for this wee man - he says,
"Yer wanted up here," he says, "we have bad news..."
His cousin it was.'
                                                'Aye.'

'Cut his throat and that was in -
then after that it was Ferguson's took it over -
I wouldn't have lived in that house!
Ferguson took it then and he opened his barber's shop in it.
But this man had a shop, like a grocer's in it.'
                                'Aye, and the mother...'
'Him and his mother - she was an old woman
and she died - wasn't it? - before him.

143

And I think that's what was wrong with him,
he missed his mother. He was an old bachelor.'
       'She was nearly one of the last that I remember
          wearing the long skirt down to the ground.'
'She wore a black skirt down to the ground
and a white apron.'
                  'And a shawl.'

'She was one of the old-fashioned ones
and she never changed her style.
I think he just pined after the mother died
because she was very good to him.'
      'That's a quare while ago - that was during the war,
                or was it?'
'After the war, just after the war.'
    'Funny enough they were saying there the other night.
      I remember that time that he committed suicide
         and it was the sensation of the town -
           everybody was talking about it.
     When you look at now and you listen to the news -
       every day it's a murder - somebody's murdered.'
'Well, do you see that day?
We couldn't take our dinner after the police left
and took the other man away. I *can't* mind his name...
That finished our Christmas dinner...'

Squincy

'Now, my husband took a squincy,
what they called squincy -
I never heard tell of...'

                                        'It's about yet.'
'Is it about yet? A squincy throat?'
    'A swelling of the throat, and it can be dangerous, like,
        if the throat closes up with it, if it's not attended to...'
'And my mother, she came over.
My husband wouldn't let me poultice it,
but he said he would let my mother.
And his throat was bad and my mother came over
and she got a shovel
and she put salt on it and there was a good fire on
and she held the shovel over the fire
until it was heated, and heated well,
and then she lifted it off. She had an old sock,
she put the salt down the sock
and she had a bottle of olive oil
and she oiled his neck, and then she...
she would have come near him gently, you know,
and, "Is that warm enough?"
till gradually he got then that he could thole it.
And then she says to me,
"I won't be over tomorrow," she says.
"Now you have been watching me
and you know what to do".
So I said, "All right, mother".
It was coming near time for it to burst anyway,
so I got on the shovel, put on the salt and all the rest of it,
and got the sock and put it in the sock
and lifted the sock and just went over
and put it on his neck. The sock hit me out at the door.
And my mother says, "Can you do nothing right -
I leave you to do anything..." And I'm telling you,
only that he couldn't speak with his throat...
you see it was rife at that time,
and it took a good wee lock to cure it, you know...'
            'I know one chap that I used to play billiards with
                        and his closed up and he died.
He was a young man about twenty-seven or twenty-eight.'
'Aye, but the poultice cured it - it burst it right enough.
She done the business every day.'

145

A Severe, Bad Night

'My father was a carpenter, but he made coffins,
and there was a man one time,
I can't remember his name, but he was a very crabbit man.
And there was a wee man they called Andy Moore.
Andy had like a Southern hard tongue.
And there was a fellow called Dan Graham
that lived down Fahan Street.
And this old crabbit man's wife died
and he asked my father to make him a coffin
and they made the coffin.
In those days they had a hand-cart
and they put the coffin on that
and wheeled it over to the Waterside there,
to where he was.
When they got to the door anyway, he was out,
and they went up
and they thought on account of working with him,
do him a good turn,
they would coffin her - she was lying on the bed.
And they coffined her.
And he came in and flew off the handle,
"Who told you to do that?"
And he reached over and he gave the corpse a shake
and the corpse's head turned round
and one eye opened, you see.
But the two boys came back,
Graham and Moore came back
and told my father
and Andy Moore, the wee hard-tongued man says,
"I declare to me God, Sam,"
that was my father's name.
"Declare to me God, Sam,
he must have been bad to her,
for when he put his hand and shook her
she looked aroun' an' opened an eye
to see who it was was for shovin' her..."
And I remember my father telling us
about a big fellow down in Walker Square,
which was down in the Long Tower at that time,
and I think he was somewhere around about six foot eight.
But the standard workhouse coffin was five foot ten -
the pauper's coffin as they called it.

But he was too big for that coffin,
so what they did was they got him to kneel.
They put the coffin up
and they stood the corpse on his knees,
bent the knees into the end of the coffin,
then they got the lid of the coffin and they all piled on,
pinned it down
and when they got it down they nailed it on.
And that man,
I don't know whether he went above or below -
on his knees...
And there was a wee man went around selling thread,
bits of yarn and stuff like that -
there was a name for them -
and he came to your house the night, you took him in,
and he got a corner to lie down next the fire,
got him fed and he went on -
a pack peddlar, that's him -
and he died.
They found him dead on the road
a very severe bad night, snow on the road,
they found wee Jimmy dead.
And they brought him in to one of the houses
and they decided to fix him up and dress him,
wake him and all.
But they had to put a stone on the chest
to try and straighten him out.
Put this big stone on the chest
and they had him over in the corner,
but before they all gathered in that night
a couple of the boyos
thought they'd play a bit of a prank on them.
They got in and put a bit of rope round the stone
and had it down the back of the bed next the wall
and they sat next to the bed
and waited till they all got in.
'And as soon as they all got in
one was saying, "Aw, Jimmy wanted to be buried
such and such a place..."
"Aw, we'll just bury him in the local place,
sure he'll not know anyway..."
"Aw, we should bury him where he wanted to be buried..."
And just at that this boy pulled the cord
and the stone rolled off him
and he shot up.
"Aw, for Jesus' sake Jimmy, lie down,
we'll bury you where you want..."

Last Rites

'Really there was never any great bother in the City.
Nineteen-twenty, now,
I remember way back to the nineteen-twenties
when there was rioting - serious rioting too -
that's when the first shooting started.
I was down - it was a Saturday night -
I was down in a wee shop at the corner, Joe Russell's,
getting something - my mother sent me down to Joe Russell's
for whatever it was she had forgot, and the shooting started.
And I remember my father coming sliding down
along the wall into Joe Russell's,
and he had me under his arm, and up into the house again.
And they moved us further down The Fountain.
They didn't leave. My father didn't leave the house,
but my mother and the brothers and sisters
were moved down to people further down
in the Lower Fountain, and we were there for a good while.
It was coming from Bishop Street and into the Long Tower,
which is opposite. I suppose it had connections
with the Rising in the South, at the time,
but they were shooting actually -
they didn't bring the Army in until after it -
it was a case of both sides at it, one side as bad as the other,
shooting at one another -
it was sectarian, definitely sectarian...'
        'Everything that happens here is sectarian -
        but people are learning a lot of sense now.
           We're Church of Ireland
        but our best friends are Roman Catholics.
And we have a friend a priest, Father Frank McLaughlin,
and Frankie always comes, because I visited his mother
    when she was sick, and the night she was dying
      the sisters all ran out of the room screaming
    and he says to me, "Margaret would you sit down
      on that side of my mother and hold that hand
    and I'll hold this hand". And I said, "Well, Frankie,
if that's what you want me to do, but maybe she'd rather
      have some of her own family doing it".
    And she said, "No...you..." and I said,
"Right, Daisy, I'll do it..." and I sat and held her hand
    while he gave her the Last Rites of the Church.
That's a long time ago - about twelve years ago...'

Crossing the Jordan

'There was a man roamed about the country,
and everybody was good to him,
he had neither kith or kin, and he was doubled a kind of -
he had a bad back. And he died
and they got a coffin made for him.
Of course the countryside gathered in.
He was bent, and to keep him down
they had to stretch him out
and they put a big stone on his feet, to keep his legs down.
Somebody in the middle of the night -
all the girls then all gathered in,
all white stockings and black boots on them -
and somebody in the middle of the night,
my father-in-law often told us,
and I could well believe it was him,
lifted the stone off the wee man's legs
and he sat up in the coffin and everybody run.
And there were what they called then 'the middins'
outside the door, mind you. And one of the girls

lived next door to my mother and she said
that they just jumped through the middin
and they were going to be murdered then
with their stockings and boots all destroyed.
A wake - that's where you went for your fun.'
                    'I remember a man coming up to my father
            at three o'clock in the morning from the Lecky Road,
                    and my father asked him what he wanted.
            "Sam," he says, "I want you to make a box."
                          "What do you mean, a box?"
                    "A box for the wee girl," he says,
              "she's just died." And he made the coffin.'
'He made them for the various undertakers.
I remember him telling us that his father
worked at the same job, and he told us that a Jew died
in the Abercorn Road, and they went down with the coffin
and put him in the coffin,
and when my father came up he said to his father,
"There was a half-a-crown in that man's hand and I took it."
And his father nearly broke his ear
and he said, "How dare you.
That was his money to cross the Jordan!"
And that was a belief that they had -
they took money in their hand for to pay for their fare
across the Jordan. And he was marched down again
to put the money back in the hand.'
                    'And there was an old fellow, a sweep,
      and they fixed him all up and his cigarette lit in his mouth
                          and they had him all dressed up
        and him sitting in the coffin and everybody coming in.
They thought nothing of it - everybody enjoyed the crack -
        augh, he was a very crabbed man in his day and then,
I suppose they were sort of getting their own back, you know.
                    And the jokes went round
        like I don't know what - there was an old couple -
they were happy enough in their own existence -
what do you call her that her man had a cart?
She was married and he had a cart that he went round with,
and he was in a pub outside Bishop's Gate.
And she shouts,"Is my Eddie in there?"
And somebody says, "Naw he's not!"
"'Deed he is, for his jeep's at the door!"
That was his jeep - the cart.'
                    'And apparently the time that the sailors were here
                    this other old character, Johnny-Cut-Thems
            was selling papers, and he was going up William Street
          and he was calling, "Press! Press!" and the sailor hit him.'

Scarletina

'As a child I took congestion on the lungs,
I was round about five and a half, six years of age.
The cure then was hot linseed poultices
and when I'm talking about hot,
I mean like the fires of hell.
And I can remember my aunt
putting those poultices on me
back and front,
and that was done three times a day.
And they were sitting up with me at night.
I wasted - I was for death - and I was in the cot ... a big cot.
And my youngest brother
was taken in to the Waterside Hospital
where the doctor had said that he'd scarletina.
And he had golden ringlets.
And my grandfather and my father were sent for
and whenever they went over, I was still there.
They were sitting up with me.
My mammy learned to snuff then.
There was an old woman, Mrs Johnston,
and she had had a stroke
and wasn't able to speak very much,
and she carried a snuff-box with her
and she used to pass the snuff-box round,
and my granny was snuffing, and my mammy was snuffing
and there were a couple of others.
And my father and my grandfather went over to the hospital
and my brother - they had cut my brother's hair...
And there was a nurse in the Waterside and she was a targer.
Nobody liked her - and James was called for my granda,
and my granda always said, "My son, didn't..."
he classed him "my son" -
"...my son didn't have no disease,
because I rubbed my hand round his face,
an' if he had the skin would have come away in my hand!"
And my brother died.
And I was lying in the cot, and my memory of him
is a hearse going down the street.
But when there was somebody ill, you sat with them
and there was always somebody was willing
to give up their night's sleep to help you
or to let you get a sleep...'